T0208921

CONSIDERING
Wisdom

Gold or Wisdom—What will it Be?

MICHAEL COPPLE

WESTBOW
PRESS®
A DIVISION OF THOMAS NELSON
& ZONDERVAN

Copyright © 2020 Michael Copple.

All rights reserved. No part of this book may be used or reproduced by any means, graphic, electronic, or mechanical, including photocopying, recording, taping or by any information storage retrieval system without the written permission of the author except in the case of brief quotations embodied in critical articles and reviews.

This book is a work of non-fiction. Unless otherwise noted, the author and the publisher make no explicit guarantees as to the accuracy of the information contained in this book and in some cases, names of people and places have been altered to protect their privacy.

WestBow Press books may be ordered through booksellers or by contacting:

WestBow Press
A Division of Thomas Nelson & Zondervan
1663 Liberty Drive
Bloomington, IN 47403
www.westbowpress.com
1 (866) 928-1240

Because of the dynamic nature of the Internet, any web addresses or links contained in this book may have changed since publication and may no longer be valid. The views expressed in this work are solely those of the author and do not necessarily reflect the views of the publisher, and the publisher hereby disclaims any responsibility for them.

Any people depicted in stock imagery provided by Getty Images are models, and such images are being used for illustrative purposes only. Certain stock imagery © Getty Images.

Scripture taken from the New King James Version®. Copyright © 1982 by Thomas Nelson. Used by permission. All rights reserved.

Scripture taken from the King James Version of the Bible.

Scripture quotations taken from The Holy Bible, New International Version® NIV® Copyright © 1973 1978 1984 2011 by Biblica, Inc. TM. Used by permission. All rights reserved worldwide.

ISBN: 978-1-9736-9622-3 (sc)
ISBN: 978-1-9736-9623-0 (hc)
ISBN: 978-1-9736-9621-6 (e)

Library of Congress Control Number: 2020913012

Print information available on the last page.

WestBow Press rev. date: 07/24/2020

TO MY GRANDDAUGHTERS

Olivette Haven Copple

Amelie Edith Copple

ACKNOWLEDGMENTS

I would like to express my deepest, genuine gratitude to the following who have contributed in so many ways to make this book possible:

First and foremost, I give thanks to our Triune God for the life-changing relationship He has given me with the Lord Jesus Christ. This new life and hope has motivated me to spread the truth of Scripture and become a true follower of our Almighty Creator.

I thank the following solid brothers in the Lord Jesus Christ who are all Spirit-gifted teachers: Randy Amos, Warren Henderson, Louis Voyer, Ed Anthony, Harold Summers, and Mike Atwood. I am extremely grateful to these brothers who've devoted so much of their lives to help us understand God's absolute truth and to better know Him and love Him by writing commentaries and speaking at conferences. Most have even come to the little assembly meeting of the Columbia Valley Bible Fellowship to bring messages that encourage the saints with growing knowledge of our Lord God and Savior.

I thank my brother in Christ and mentor, Ralph Kirchhofer, who has further developed my walk with the Lord. For the past thirteen years, Ralph has encouraged me moment by moment to take on more responsibilities, especially to spread the Gospel. He has often reminded and instilled in me that "in all things the Lord Jesus Christ may have the preeminence."

Those at WestBow Press, such as John, Jeanine, DeeAnna, Bob, and the ones behind the scenes in the printing and corrections departments, have once again made it a wonderful, encouraging experience to get to know them and work with them.

I thank my loving wife, Elfriede Copple, who has actually worked longer and harder than I did to write this book. Elfriede's gifts of administration and long-suffering were incalculable for communicating with the WestBow publishing staff, and for her labors to edit, market, and design the cover, I give her my heartfelt, deep appreciation. She and I both hope this book will make a positive impact for the Lord's purpose. To God be the glory.

Finally, I thank my dad and mom for instilling a foundation of patriotism, moral values, and faith, and for the way they raised my brother and sisters and myself with unfailing love and energy. I would not be the person I am today without what they did for me.

INTRODUCTION

Quoted Scriptures are indented, and brackets within the quotes are the author's accompaniment for further explanation.

The purpose of *Considering Wisdom* is not to divulge wisdom; rather, it is to consider wisdom in all our thoughts, discernment, decisions, actions, and reactions. Furthermore, the purpose is to develop a hunger for the Book that does convey wisdom: the Bible. *Considering Wisdom* can in no way profess to impart wisdom or compare to explain wisdom like the library of Books that does: the Holy Bible, and especially the Book within the Bible titled Proverbs. The Book of Proverbs is primarily focused on wisdom. The Bible consists of sixty-six Books, all of which are inspired by the Source of wisdom—our God and Creator.

> All Scripture is given by inspiration of God.
> (2 Timothy 3:16a)

Since some chapters apply to special interest groups who are only inquisitive about their area of discussion, important points will be repeated from previous chapters so that these readers will not miss out on basic but essential reasons to consider wisdom that is relative to all concerned.

CONTENTS

Chapter 1
WISDOM VERSUS KNOWLEDGE

In terms of times and ages, the longest word in our language is the word *eternity*. Astoundingly, when we consider how the longest, endless running major rivers on six of Earth's seven continents contribute greatly to wisdom, it can lead to other far-reaching magnificent truths. Considering wisdom's eternal consequences, a list of only a few of the world's famous rivers will serve well to reveal how wisdom and nature are supernaturally linked:

Asia	Chang (Yangtze) River	3,434 miles (5,530 km) long
Australia	Murray-Darling River	2,310 miles (3,720 km) long
Europe	Volga River	2,290 miles (3,700 km) long
North America	Missouri River	2,540 miles (4,090 km) long
North America	Mississippi River	2,340 miles (3,770 km) long
South America	Amazon River	4,157 miles (6,694 km) long
Africa	Nile River	3,915 miles (6,305 km) long[1]

Other famous rivers:

Columbia River	Canada/United States
St. Lawrence River	Canada
Elbe River	Germany

---

[1] EnchantedLearning.com – Major Rivers of the World, (accessed June 2019), https://www.enchantedlearning.com/geography/rivers/majorrivers.shtml

Rhein River	Switzerland/Liechtenstein/Austria/France/Germany/Netherlands
Mosel River	France/Luxembourg/Germany
Ohio River	United States
Arkansas River	United States
Potomac River	United States

Since there are 165 famous rivers in the world, these lists are by no means near complete. These rivers seem to flow forever; year after year, day and night. By applying wisdom, we can see that's a lot of continuous water flowing. With examination of the evidence, it becomes more fully understood, beyond simply nature's implications to supernatural certainties. Knowing these facts contributes to wisdom.

To maintain perspective, some of the world's largest waterfalls are listed:

Victoria Falls	Zimbabwe/Zambia 1 mile (1.7 km) wide, 360 feet (108 meters) high
Angel Falls	Salto Angel, Venezuela dropping a total of 978 meters from the summit (3,230 feet high; uninterrupted drop: 2,647 feet)
Niagara Falls	United States/Canada (most visited tourist attraction in the world)
Kaieteur Falls	Potano River, Guyana 663 cubic meters of water per second (23,400 cubic feet/second)
Yosemite Falls	Yosemite National Park, California (tallest waterfall in the United States)[2]
Gullfoss Falls	Hvita, Iceland
Jog Falls	Created by River Sharavathi in India
Plitvice Waterfalls	Plitvice Lakes National Park, Croatia
Sutherland Falls	New Zealand
Tugela Falls	South Africa

---

[2]   17 Greatest Waterfalls in the World, #12 Yosemite Falls, Touropia.com (June 2019) https://www.touropia.com/greatest-waterfalls-in-the-world/

Nohkalikai Falls	Himalayas of India
Dettifoss Falls	Vatnajokull National Park, Iceland
Takakaw Falls	Yoho National Park, Canada
Gocta Cataracts Falls	Peru
Huangguoshu Falls	Asia
Detian Falls	Border of China and Vietnam
Blue Nile Falls	Northern Ethiopia

"Few geographical features exemplify the beauty and power of nature [or creation] as dramatically as majestic waterfalls. The sight of tons of water spilling over the edge of a cliff or cascading over rocks never fails to impress."[3]

The enormous power of these waterfalls is enough to generate electrical power for metropolitan cities as well as massive rural areas. The Kaieteur Falls of the Potano River in Guyana, cited above, producing 663 cubic meters of water every second, equal to 23,413.6 cubic feet per second.

The weight density of only one cubic foot water is 62.4 pounds.[4]

Just imagine a square container, one foot wide, one foot long, and one foot high, filled with water. The weight of the water filling that container is 62.4 pounds. Now multiply that cubic weight of 23,413.6 × 62.4 and realize that there are 1,461,008 pounds of water spilling out of that waterfall *every second*. That is about 44,000 tons of water each minute, about 2.5 million tons every hour—about 60 million tons of water running nonstop, day after day. And that's from only one waterfall in South America.

What is it that causes the ocean to maintain its constant level, even though all these waterfalls and rivers continuously feed it?

---

[3] 17 Greatest Waterfalls in the World, 1st paragraph, Touropia.com (June 2019) https://www.touropia.com/greatest-waterfalls-in-the-world/

[4] search aqua-calc.com, #compounds, site owner AVCalc LLC, (July 2019) https://www.aqua-calc.com/calculate/volume-to-weight

All the rivers run into the sea, yet the sea is not full; to the place from which the rivers come, there they return again. (Ecclesiastes 1:7)

Ecclesiastes was written nearly three thousand years ago (circa 930 BC), likely by King Solomon of Israel, son and successor of King David. God had answered Solomon's prayer for wisdom:

"Therefore give Your servant an understanding heart to judge Your people, that I may discern between good and evil. For who is able to judge this great people of Yours?" The speech pleased the Lord, that Solomon had asked this thing. Then God said to him, "Because you have asked this thing, and have not asked long life for yourself, nor have asked riches for yourself, nor have asked the life of your enemies, but have asked for yourself understanding to discern justice, behold, I have done according to your words; see, I have given you a wise and understanding heart, so that there has not been anyone like you before you, nor shall any like you arise after you." (1 Kings 3:9–12)

God blessed Solomon with more wisdom than any other earthly natural person. And God's Spirit inspired Solomon to write this:

The fear of the LORD is the beginning of wisdom, and the knowledge of the Holy One is understanding. (Proverbs 9:10)

Fear is not necessarily being afraid. In this case, "the fear of the Lord" is trusting Him, respecting Him, and having faith in Him. The original Hebrew word for *fear* in Proverbs 9:10 is *yirâh*, which translates to "being reverent"; that is, giving awesome respect. It's not about being afraid.[5]

---

[5]   James Strong, *The New Strong's Expanded Exhaustive Concordance of the Bible* (Thomas Nelson, 2001), s.v. "fear"

Philosophy is the quest for knowledge and wisdom. In Greek, philosophy is philosophia, which literally means "love of wisdom," from philos, love, and sophia, wisdom. Philosophy is then further defined as "the science which aims at an explanation of all the phenomena of the universe by ultimate causes."[6]

Warren Henderson, author of The Beginning of Wisdom (a fourteen-volume devotional commentary series encompassing the entire Old Testament), comments on Proverbs:

> True wisdom is inseparable from the fear of the Lord; it is man's starting point in understanding the mind of God and enables him to resolve questions otherwise inscrutable. Those who heed Wisdom's invitation will find life and blessing, but those who do not will be responsible for their own destruction (9:11–12). … When fallen human nature is forbidden to do a certain thing, that prohibition stirs up the desire to do it all the more (Rom. 7:7–8). Hence, the sensual invitation of the provocative woman is quite enticing to the inherent wanton instinct of the young man.[7]
>
> For the commandment is a lamp, and the law a light; reproofs of instruction are the way of life, to keep you from the evil woman, from the flattering tongue of a seductress. Do not lust after her beauty in your heart, nor let her allure you with her eyelids. For by means of a harlot a man is reduced to a crust of bread; and an adulteress will prey upon his precious life. (Proverbs 6:23–26)

Henderson continues, "One learns through experience that pursuing temporary pleasure leads to death and misery. May we too count the long-term cost of sin and choose to abide with the Lord in His wisdom."[8]

---

[6] Consolidated Book Publishers Chicago, *The New Webster Encyclopedic Dictionary of the English Language* (Processing & Books, Inc.), s.v. "philosphy"

[7] Warren Henderson, *The Beginning of Wisdom*, pg 373—ISBN 978-1-939770-30-1 (2016)

[8] Warren Henderson, *The Beginning of Wisdom*, pg 373—ISBN 978-1-939770-30-1 (2016)

People say that the ocean is rising or is going to rise, one of many claims that God stirs us to question:

> It is better to trust in the LORD than to put confidence in man. It is better to trust in the LORD than to put confidence in princes. (Psalm 118:8–9)

"Not only the earth, the sun, and the wind, but the water has followed its same repetitive routine throughout the centuries. All the rivers run into the sea but never to the point where the ocean overflows, because the sun evaporates enormous quantities of water. Then as air cools, the vapor condenses and forms clouds. The clouds in turn scud across the skies and drop the water over the land areas in the form of rain, snow, or hail. And as the rivers are fed with the surplus, they bear the water back to the ocean."[9]

> That which has been is what will be, that which is done is what will be done, and there is nothing new under the sun. (Ecclesiastes 1:9)

> That which is has already been, and what is to be has already been. (Ecclesiastes 3:15a)

This hydro cycle replenishes the earth's water supply—enough to water vegetation; satisfy the thirst of wildlife, domestic animals, and humans; stock up springs; water lawns, gardens and flower beds; flush toilets; drain bathtubs and showers; and still refill the rivers. Sometimes, the weather cycles down to drought condition, but other times, it delivers so much rain that floods occur. There is definitely a balance. To combine this knowledge with wisdom, what wisdom can we obtain from these powerful, majestic rivers and falls?

Contemplating the volume of water emptied into the oceans by the earth's rivers along with all the sunken ocean liners, warships, and

---

[9]   William MacDonald, *Believer's Bible Commentary*, (Thomas Nelson, 1995), pg 881 (commentary on Ecclesiastes 1:7)

icebergs, it is quite incredible that the oceans do not rise. The shorelines remain where they were in Old Testament times.

Proponents of global warming bank much of their argument on icebergs melting. But the very reason ice cubes float on top of a glass of water is because ice weighs less than water. "One cubic ft of ice weighs 57.4 pounds. That's exactly 5 pounds less than one cubic ft of water."[10]

Simply put, if a glass is half-full of water, and ice cubes are added to fill the glass, and the glass is left undisturbed to allow the ice to melt, then the glass will no longer be full. Additionally, applying wisdom, it's interesting to note that icebergs fall off and melt only in the spring and summer of the Northern or Southern Hemispheres. Being cyclic with weather conditions, they build up again in the fall and winter. If this cycle did not occur, it seems reasonable to assume the ice would continue to grow infinitely.

With wisdom in the equation, we see that it would be easy to be deceived if one falls for changing sea levels in various places. If the ocean is said to be rising in one isolated place, then it should equally have risen across the globe. "While changes in storminess may contribute to changes in sea level extremes, the limited geographical coverage of studies to date and the uncertainties associated with storminess changes overall mean that a general assessment of the effects of storminess changes on storm surge is not possible at this time."[11]

Applying wisdom, the conclusion at this point is clearly seen that sea levels can appear to increase and decrease in various places depending upon weather cycles.

China recently pumped enough material into the ocean to create islands large enough to support military bases with aircraft landing strips. "In

---

[10] search aqua-calc.com, "compounds" – 1 cubic foot of solid ice, site owner AVCalc LLC, (July 2019) https://www.aqua-calc.com/calculate/volume-to-weight

[11] Centre for Climate Adaptation, ClimateChangePost, Iceland, "Extreme water levels – Global trends", last sentence in 1st paragraph, (July 2019) https://www. climatechangepost.com/iceland/coastal-floods/

2015, China began pumping sand onto disputed reefs in the (sovereignty disputed) Spratly Island group of the South China Sea. Three years later, what used to be partially submerged coral features are now fully fledged islands, hosting buildings, ports, and runways."[12]

The Spratly Islands are located approximately five hundred miles due east of Ho Chi Minh (Saigon), in the southern part of Vietnam.

Not all the materials on the islands are new to the ocean; the Chinese moved some of the sediment from the seafloor to the reefs. However, the port facilities, buildings, and airstrips add new weights to the ocean. This should be taken into consideration as we continue examining the evidence to achieve wisdom.

"The speed and scale of China's island-building spree have alarmed other countries with interests in the region. China announced in June that the creation of islands—moving sediment from the seafloor to a reef—would soon be completed. Since then, China has focused its efforts on construction. So far it has constructed port facilities, military buildings and an airstrip on the islands, with recent imagery showing evidence of two more airstrips under construction."[13]

There is a division among scientists who believe in human-made global warming / climate change and those who claim it is a deception. The faction does not stop with scientists. A number of journalists and their sources of news on the subject are also in disagreement. Some declare that 97 percent of all scientists agree that humans are causing the climate to change, while other sources say that over thirty-one thousand scientists have signed a petition that human-made climate change is a hoax.

---

[12] THE DIPLOMAT, "China's Build-Up: The View From Space" July 11, 2018, 1st paragraph, (June 2019) https://thediplomat.com/2018/07/chinas-island-build-up-the-view-from-space/

[13] The New York Times, "What China Has Been Building in the South China Sea" October 27, 2015, 2nd paragraph – 1st three sentences, (June 2019) https://www.nytimes.com/interactive/2015/07/30/world/asia/what-china-has-been-building-in-the-south-china-sea.html

Alex Epstein, a contributor to *Forbes* magazine, wrote the article "'97% of Climate Scientists Agree' is 100% Wrong."He wrote: "If you've ever expressed the least bit of skepticism about environmentalist calls for making the vast majority of fossil fuel use illegal, you've probably heard the smug response: "97% of climate scientists agree with climate change" — which always carries the implication: Who are you to challenge them? The answer is: you are a thinking, independent individual--and you don't go by polls, let alone second-hand accounts of polls; you go by facts, logic and explanation."[14]

"More than 31,000 American scientists (to date) have signed a petition challenging the climate change narrative and 9,029 of them hold PhDs in their respective fields."[15] Retired senior NASA atmospheric scientist John L. Casey claimed that solar cycles are largely responsible for warming periods on Earth—not human activity.

The Heritage Foundation quoted the following report by the US Government Accountability Office: "Federal funding for climate change research, technology, international assistance, and adaptation has increased from $2.4 billion in 1993 to $11.6 billion in 2014, with an additional $26.1 billion for climate change programs and activities provided by the American Recovery and Reinvestment Act in 2009." [16] This doesn't solve the controversy of whether or not the planet is warming. "But the tidal wave of funding does reveal a powerful financial motive for scientists to conclude that the apocalypse is upon us."[17]

---

[14] Forbes Media LLC, January 6, 2015, article by Alex Epstein "'97% Of Climat Scientists Agree' Is 100% Wrong" 1st and 2nd paragraph, (June 2019) https://www.forbes.com/sites/alexepstein/2015/01/06/97-of-climate-scientists-agree-is-100-wrong/#45c65db93f9f

[15] TBU News, August 31, 2016, Earth and Nature, article by Daniel Barker "Man-Made Global Warming a complete hoax and science lie?" 14th paragraph, (June 2019) https://tbunews.com/man-made-global-warming-a-complete-hoax-and-science-lie

[16] The Heritage Foundation-Commentary- Environment-December 18, 2018 by Stephen Moore "Follow the (Climate Change) Money", 3rd paragraph, (June 2019) https://www.heritage.org/environment/commentary/follow-the-climate-change-money

[17] The Heritage Foundation-Commentary- Environment-December 18, 2018 by Stephen Moore "Follow the (Climate Change) Money", 4th paragraph, (June 2019) https://www.heritage.org/environment/commentary/follow-the-climate-change-money

The world does continue to have huge debates over climate change reports. It goes along well with what the Lord Jesus said would happen as we near the beginning of the end:

> "Take heed that no one deceives you. For many will come in My name, saying, 'I am the Christ,' and will deceive many. And you will hear of wars and rumors of wars. See that you are not troubled; for all these things must come to pass, but the end is not yet. For nation will rise against nation, and kingdom against kingdom. And there will be famines, pestilences, and earthquakes in various places. All these are the beginning of sorrows" (Matthew 24:4b–8).

The NIV compares the last sentence, verse 8, to a pregnant woman's pains in the beginning stages of giving birth:

> "All these are the beginning of birth pains."
> (Matthew 24:8 NIV).

Kept in context, the passage goes on with the Savior's explanation of what will take place after He takes His believers up to be with Him: There will be a seven-year tribulation period for those unbelievers who will be left behind. Revelation 1:3b tells us,

> "The time is near." (Revelation 1:3b)

When we read the Lord Jesus' words "various places," it reminds us not to go into a "state of fear" if storms like Hurricane Sandy cause the sea to overflow, like it did in New Jersey. It should be noted that the water receded soon after the storm. The same can be said for the "storminess" that took place in Iceland. It is wise to take heed of Jesus' words in the Matthew 24 passage:

> "Take heed that no one deceives you." (Matthew 24:4b)

If someone posts a picture of an automobile submerged up to its windows on a beach and claims the ocean is rising, do not be deceived. Ask the question, "Was the car parked there during low tide and the photo made at high tide?"

If you see a magazine article with pictures of large glaciers above lush green vegetation with the caption, "This is what it used to be," and then a comparison with the same glacier half-melted away above dry, brown desert-looking terrain with the caption, "This is what it looks like twenty years later," do not be deceived. The first photo was likely taken in the spring before summer melting occurred, and the second taken in late August or early September. Even if there were twenty years' difference, seasonal differences are quite normal every year. Be careful. Do not be deceived.

While both sides may be right in that the climate does change (which it has been doing in cycles for hundreds and thousands of years), their differences are based upon claims for what the causes are of the more catastrophic climate events. What wisdom can we attain from all this? The One with whom to reason is the Creator—the Lord GOD Himself.

> The fear of the LORD is the beginning of wisdom,
> a good understanding have all those who do His
> commandments. (Psalm 111:10a)

> A wise man will hear and increase learning, and a man
> of understanding will attain wise counsel. (Proverbs 1:5)

Although many people dismiss claims that the entire earth was once flooded, knowledge and wisdom give reason to pause and consider: It's noteworthy to acknowledge that fish fossils have been found on Mount Everest, the highest mountain in the world. Climbers who have been to the top of Mount Everest brought back rocks that contained the fossils of sea lilies.[18]

---

[18] The Times of India, "Why Are There Fish Fossils High Up In The Himalayas?" by Mishana Khot – 29 June 2018, 2nd paragraph – last sentence. (June 2019) https://weather.com/en-IN/india/news/news/2018-06-29-fish-fossil-himalayas

Of course, people could attempt to explain this by saying that the fish were there before the mountains were folded and then the continents were separated and formed. But God saw this argument coming and provides a sound explanation. Do not become discouraged. Read and compare the following verses, from Genesis:

> In the beginning God created the heavens and the earth.

> The earth was without form, and void; and darkness was on the face of the deep. And the Spirit of God was hovering over the face of the waters....

> Then God said, "Let there be a firmament in the midst of the waters, and let it divide the waters from the waters." (Genesis 1:1–2, 6)

That was the second day.

The waters were divided on the second day, creating the continents of the earth. But the living creatures, including the living creatures of the sea were not created until after the fourth day—after the continents were separated by the oceans:

> So the evening and the morning were the fourth day. (Genesis 1:19)

Then on the fifth day:

> Then God said, "Let the waters abound with an abundance of living creatures, and let birds fly above the earth across the face of the firmament of the heavens." (Genesis 1:20)

Then, on the sixth day, man was created. After that, for the next sixteen hundred years, humankind multiplied. Then people became so wicked that God destroyed all people on the earth with a flood—except for Noah and seven others of his family, who survived:

Then the LORD saw that the wickedness of man was great in the earth, and that every intent of the thoughts of his heart was only evil continually. And the LORD was sorry that He had made man on the earth, and He was grieved in His heart. (Genesis 6:5–6)

Now the flood was on the earth forty days. The waters increased and lifted up the ark, and it rose high above the earth…. And the waters prevailed exceedingly on the earth, and all the high hills under the whole heaven were covered. The waters prevailed fifteen cubits upward, and the mountains were covered. (Genesis 7:17, 20)

The mountains were formed on the fourth day of creation, but the flood did not occur until sixteen hundred and fifty years later. The fish fossils that were created on the fifth day, being found on Mount Everest, provide clear evidence that the earth was totally under water.

Wisdom points us to trusting that God is in control. Concerning the enormous amount of water that flows from all the rivers into the ocean, the Author of the Bible, God Himself, says:

Or who shut the sea with doors, when it burst forth and issued from the womb; when I made the clouds its garment, and thick darkness its swaddling band; when I fixed My limit for it, and set the bars and doors; when I said, "This far you may come, but no farther, and here your proud waves must stop!" (Job 38:8–11)

It does not stop there. When God speaks, we can rest assured it is important. When He says it twice, which we've now seen with Ecclesiastes 1:7 and Job 38:8–11, it is definitely worth listening to. And when He says it three or four or even five times, we are prompted to give it our utmost attention:

You who laid the foundations of the earth, so that it should not be moved forever, You covered it with the deep as with a garment; the waters stood above the mountains. At Your rebuke they fled; at the voice of Your thunder they hastened away. They went up over the mountains; they went down into the valleys, to the place which You founded for them. You have set a boundary that they may not pass over, that they may not return to cover the earth. (Psalm 104:5–9)

When He assigned to the sea its limit, so that the waters would not transgress His command, when he marked out the foundations of the earth. (Proverbs 8:29)

"Do you not fear Me?" says the LORD. "Will you not tremble at My presence, who have placed the sand as the bound of the sea, by a perpetual decree, that it cannot pass beyond it? And though its waves toss to and fro, yet they cannot prevail; though they roar, yet they cannot pass over it." (Jeremiah 5:22)

Admittedly, it is difficult for us to believe the whole earth was flooded since we, in our lifetime, have not seen it happen. Why wouldn't it reoccur? Because our Creator promised to never flood the entire earth again. God does not break His promises.

Then God spoke to Noah and to his sons with him, saying: "And as for Me, behold, I establish My covenant with you and with your descendants after you, and with every living creature that is with you: the birds, the cattle, and every beast of the earth with you, of all that go out of the ark, every beast of the earth. Thus I establish My covenant with you: Never again shall all flesh be cut off by the waters of the flood; never again shall there be a flood to destroy the earth." And God said: "This is the sign of the covenant which I make between Me and you, and every living creature that is with you, for perpetual generations: I set My rainbow in the cloud, and it shall be for the sign of the covenant between Me and the earth.

It shall be, when I bring a cloud over the earth, that the rainbow shall be seen in the cloud; and I will remember My covenant which is between Me and you and every living creature of all flesh; the waters shall never again become a flood to destroy all flesh." (Genesis 9:8–15)

W. E. Vine describes *wisdom* as "the ability to discern modes of action with a view to their results."[19] (In layman's terms: looking ahead to see the consequences of one's decisions.)

"Wisdom: The right use or exercise of knowledge; the choice of laudable ends and the best means to accomplish them. Wisdom differs somewhat from *prudence*, in this respect: *prudence* is the exercise of sound judgment in avoiding evils; *wisdom* is the exercise of sound judgment either in avoiding evils or attempting good. *Prudence* then is a species, of which *wisdom* is the genus."[20]

Where is the wise?… Has not God made foolish the wisdom of this world? (1 Corinthians 1:20a, c)

But God has chosen the foolish things of the world to put to shame the wise, and God has chosen the weak things of the world to put to shame the things which are mighty. (1 Corinthians 2:27)

And to man He said, "Behold, the fear of the Lord, that is wisdom, and to depart from evil is understanding." (Job 28:28)

Since God has kept His promise to never flood the earth again and maintain the boundaries of the ocean, rational thinking leads us to further investigate His omnipotent power—beyond nature—and delve into our very human minds, souls, and spirits.

---

19 *Vine's Expository Dictionary of Old & New Testament Words*, (Thomas Nelson 1996), pg 1233 s.v. "wisdom" (June 2019)
20 The original *American Dictionary of the English Language*, Noah Webster, 1828, s.v. "wisdom"

Chapter 2
COMMON SENSE OF WISDOM

To have common sense, a person must be able to make good judgments and to have sound reasoning ability.

> "Come now, and let us reason together," says the LORD.
> (Isaiah 1:18a)

God is indeed in control of the weather, which in turn determines the hydro cycle that was explained in the first chapter. The next chapter, backed up with Scripture, confirms God is the Creator of the universe, this planet, and everything on it, and He undeniably controls the earth's weather. Having the freedom to reason with our very Creator would not only be using common sense, but it would also be an absolute privilege.

The following verses teach us about the earth's weather and are definitely worth looking up and reading: Job 36:26–33, 37:1–18, 38:1–11, 22–38; Psalm 89:9, 104:6–9, 147:16–18, Jeremiah 10:12–13, 14:22, 31:35, 51:15–16; Joel 2:23; Amos 5:7–8; Matthew 5:45; Mark 4:39; and Acts 14:15–17. To be sure, He who created this earth is in control of the weather. We are not.

The Bible has many other intriguing characteristics: For instance, the center chapter of the Bible is Psalm 118. Immediately preceding Psalm 118 is the shortest chapter in the Bible: Psalm 117, with only two verses. The chapter immediately following Psalm 118 is Psalm 119, with the most verses: 160 verses. It's fascinating to note that there are exactly

1,188 chapters before Psalm 118 and exactly 1,188 chapters afterward. It's overwhelming and worth repeating that Psalm 118:8, in the center of the God's Word, gives that incredible wisdom to trust in the Lord rather than having confidence in man.

Nonetheless, our pride, that is, avoiding conviction of guilt and fearing peer pressure, still motivates us to reject the truth:

> Nevertheless even among the rulers many believed in Him [believed in Jesus being the Son of God], but because of the Pharisees they did not confess Him, lest they should be put out of the synagogue; for they loved the praise of men more than the praise of God. (John 12:42–43)

Jesus said,

> "For whoever is ashamed of Me and My words in this adulterous and sinful generation, of him the Son of Man also will be ashamed when He comes in the glory of His Father with the holy angels" (Mark 8:38; Luke 9:26).

It's been well said, "I would rather stand with God and be judged by the world than to stand with the world and be judged by God."

For nearly sixteen hundred years, over forty writers were inspired by the Holy Spirit to write what became the Bible, yet the entirety of the sixty-six Books are miraculously in perfect agreement. There are no contradictions. The reason:

> All Scripture is given by inspiration of God. (2 Timothy 3:16a)

> For we did not follow cunningly devised fables when we made known to you the power and coming of our Lord Jesus Christ, but were eyewitnesses of His Majesty. (2 Peter 1:16)

> Knowing this first, that no prophecy of Scripture is of any private interpretation, for prophecy never came by the will of man, but holy men of God spoke as they were moved by the Holy Spirit. (2 Peter 1:20–21)

Scripture compared to Scripture reinforces its immutability and endurance, and confirms its flawlessness, perfection, continuity, and truth.

> Every word of God is pure [tested, refined, flawless]; He is a shield to those who put their trust in Him. Do not add to His words, lest He rebuke you, and you be found a liar. (Proverbs 30:5–6)

The fantastic, supernatural power that God performed means more than all else: He sent His Son from heaven to earth to dwell among us and to shed His blood to forgive whoever believes in Him and for Him to die, taking the offenders' punishment so that believers could have life. And He raised Him from the dead, showing that He has the power to raise the dead and to give people hope for everlasting life.

Some have a problem believing this could possibly be true, but when we consider that He is also the Creator of everything we see, then we can surmise it is not insurmountable.

> But Jesus looked at them and said to them, "With men this is impossible, but with God all things are possible." (Matthew 19:26)

Forty days after being resurrected from the dead, eleven of His disciples saw Him ascend up into the clouds:

> Until the day in which He was taken up, after He through the Holy Spirit had given commandments to the apostles whom He had chosen, to whom He also presented Himself alive after His suffering by many infallible [unmistakable] proofs, being seen by

them during forty days and speaking of the things pertaining to the kingdom of God.... Now when He had spoken these things, while they watched, He was taken up, and a cloud received Him out of their sight. (Acts 1:2–3, 9)

In our temporary life here on earth, we see rapid changes taking place.

In roughly five hundred years before the in-the-flesh birth of the eternal past, present, and future God, our Savior, the Greek philosopher Heraclitus got it wrong when he made his following statement about change: "There is nothing permanent except change." Other philosophers who followed him later in time: Socrates, Plato, Aristotle, and others have changed the wording to say something more along this line: "The only thing that does not change ... is change itself." However, they all missed an extremely important point, which had already been written two hundred years before Heraclitus was even born. Written in about 700 BC, Isaiah was inspired by the Spirit of God to write:

The grass withers, the flower fades, but the word of our God stands forever. (Isaiah 40:8; 1 Peter 1:24b–25)

For I am the LORD, I do not change. (Malachi 3:6)

The reason God's Word endures forever is because He Himself does not change. In regard to all those early philosophers, about six hundred years later, Paul the apostle wrote,

"Has not God made foolish the wisdom of this world?" (1 Corinthians 1:20b).

It just makes common sense to want to obtain wisdom. In a way, wisdom equates to common sense, but God's wisdom far surpasses common sense. With such a powerful, all-knowing, everlasting God, it just makes plain, good reasoning to consider His wisdom. Psalm 139, verses 1 to 16, points out that God is omniscient; He is knowledgeable of everything past, present, or future that He created or will create. He is also omnipresent beyond our comprehension; He is present everywhere at all times. And He is omnipotent in that He has the power to do anything He pleases, even to raise the dead.

God's Omniscience

> O LORD, You have searched me and known me. You know my sitting down and my rising up; You understand my thought afar off. You comprehend my path and my lying down, and are acquainted with all my ways. For there is not a word on my tongue, but behold, O LORD, You know it altogether. You have hedged me behind and before, and laid Your hand upon me. Such knowledge is too wonderful for me; it is high, I cannot attain it. (Psalm 139:1–6)

> But Jesus, knowing their thoughts, said, "Why do you think evil in your hearts?" (Matthew 9:4)

> But immediately, when Jesus perceived in His spirit that they reasoned thus within themselves, He said to them, "Why do you reason about these things in your hearts?" (Mark 2:8)

> I, the LORD, search the heart, I test the mind, even to give every man according to his ways, according to the fruit of his doings. (Jeremiah 17:10)

> Hear, O earth! Behold, I will certainly bring calamity on this people—the fruit of their thoughts, because they have not heeded My words nor My law, but rejected it. (Jeremiah 6:19)

When we pray to God and sincerely ask for forgiveness, we don't even have to say it audibly. He knows our thoughts. However, it is greatly encouraging to other believers to be able to agree with other's prayers and hear the prayer of a new believer who'll be joining them in God's everlasting kingdom.

God's Omnipresence

> Where can I go from Your Spirit? Or where can I flee from Your presence? If I ascend into heaven, You are there; If I make my bed in hell [or Shēōl, Hādēs], behold, You are there. If I take the wings of the morning, and dwell in the uttermost parts of the sea, even there Your hand shall lead me, and Your right hand shall hold me. If I say, "Surely the darkness shall fall on me," even the night shall be light about me; indeed, the darkness shall not hide from You, but the night shines as the day; the darkness and the light are both alike to You. (Psalm 139:7–12)

> The LORD looks down from heaven; He sees all the sons of men. From the place of His dwelling He looks on all the inhabitants of the earth; He fashions their hearts individually; He considers all their works. (Psalm 33:13–15)

> You have set our iniquities [sins, disobedience, offenses] before You, our secret sins in the light of Your countenance. (Psalm 90:8)

> "Am I a God near at hand," says the LORD, "And not a God afar off? Can anyone hide himself in secret places, so I shall not see him?" says the LORD; "Do I not fill heaven and earth?" says the LORD. (Jeremiah 23:23–24)

> And there is no creature hidden from His sight, but all things are naked and open to the eyes of Him to whom we must give account. (Hebrews 4:13)

God's Omnipotence

For You formed my inward parts; You covered me in my mother's womb. I will praise You, for I am fearfully and wonderfully made; marvelous are Your works, and that my soul knows very well. My frame was not hidden from You, when I was made in secret, and skillfully wrought in the lowest parts of the earth. Your eyes saw my substance, being yet unformed. And in Your book they all were written, the days fashioned for me, when as yet there were none of them. (Psalm 139:13–16)

Thus says the LORD who made you and formed you from the womb, who will help you. (Isaiah 44:2a)

Thus says the LORD your Redeemer, and He who formed you from the womb: "I am, the LORD, who makes all things, who stretches out the heavens all alone, who spreads abroad the earth by Myself; who frustrates the signs of the babblers, and drives diviners mad; who turns wise men backward, and makes their knowledge foolishness." (Isaiah 44:24–25)

For by Him [Jesus] all things were created that are in heaven and that are on earth, visible and invisible, whether thrones or dominions or principalities or powers. All things were created through Him and for Him. And He is before all things, and in Him all things consist. (Colossians 1:16–17)

All things were made through Him [Jesus], and without Him nothing was made that was made. (John 1:3)

But if the Spirit of Him who raised Jesus from the dead dwells in you, He who raised Christ from the dead will also give life to your mortal bodies through His Spirit who dwells in you. (Romans 8:11)

And God both raised up the Lord and will also raise us up by His power. (1 Corinthians 6:14)

Knowing that He who raised up the Lord Jesus will also raise us up with Jesus, and will present us with you. (2 Corinthians 4:14)

All people will be raised up from death for judgment—either at the judgment seat of Christ when He will reward believers for serving Him or at the Great White Throne for judgment, when He will determine what degree of punishment the unbelievers will receive in the eternal Lake of Fire. The only way to avoid that penalty is to admit to God and sincerely ask His forgiveness for the offenses we have committed, believe the Savior took the punishment for us, and believe without doubting that we can also be raised from the dead.

Jesus said to him [Thomas], "I am the way, the truth and the life. No one comes to the Father except through Me" (John 14:6).

When statements are made that seem questionable to our human intellect, we often hear the advice: "Consider the source." Where does wisdom come from?

Chapter 3
CONSIDER THE SOURCE

This statement is often heard after an eyebrow-raising report has been announced: "Consider the source." People often try to influence the opinions of others by bogus means of deception. The result can leave the listener in doubt and devalue the speaker's integrity. Truth must be upheld to preserve integrity.

Jesus said, "For this cause I was born, and for this cause I have come into the world, that I should bear witness to the truth." (John 18:37b)

Both of the Father and of Christ in whom are hidden all the treasures of wisdom and knowledge. (Colossians 2:2b–3)

Christ Jesus, who became for us wisdom from God. (1 Corinthians 1:30a)

From where then does wisdom come? And where is the place of understanding? It is hidden from the eyes of all living, and concealed from the birds of the air. Destruction and Death say, "We have heard a report about it with our ears." God understands its way, and He knows its place. For He looks to the ends of the earth, and sees under the whole heavens, to establish a weight for the wind, and apportion the waters by measure.

When He made a law for the rain, and a path for the thunderbolt, then He saw wisdom and declared it; He prepared it, indeed, He searched it out. And to man He said, "Behold, the fear of the Lord, that is wisdom, and to depart from evil is understanding." (Job 28:20–28)

The Book of Job, likely written between 2100 and 1700 BC, is probably the oldest Book in the Bible. Before the Scriptures were written, wisdom was hidden from our eyes, but now, we obtain wisdom from God through His inspired Words in the completed Holy Bible.

God, the Foundation of all wisdom, the Source of wisdom, has not been acknowledged by scientists: *On the Origin of Species, The Boiling Point, The Heat Is On*, and *An Inconvenient Truth* all ignore and contradict the library of wisdom and truth: the Holy Bible. The Bible consists of sixty-six Books that provide guidance for God's truth, our belief, our values, and His invitation for our rescue from eternal suffering to eternal life. This Good Book is what imparts wisdom upon our souls.

We've all heard these famous statements: "Only two things are for sure: death and taxes," and "No one of gets out of here alive." The Scriptures make it clear:

The days of our lives are seventy years; and if by reason of strength they are eighty years, yet their boast is only labor and sorrow; for it is soon cut off, and we fly away. Who knows the power of Your anger? For as the fear of You, so is Your wrath. So teach us to number our days, that we may gain a heart of wisdom. (Psalm 90:10–12)

Therefore, just as through one man [Adam] sin entered the world, and death through sin, and thus death spread to all men, because all sinned. (Romans 5:12)

And as it is appointed for men to die once, but after this the judgment. (Hebrews 9:27)

For the wages of sin is death, but the gift of God is eternal life in Christ Jesus our Lord. (Romans 6:23)

See then that you walk circumspectly, not as fools but as wise, redeeming the time, because the days are evil. Therefore do not be unwise, but understand what the will of the Lord is. (Ephesians 5:15–17)

For the message of the cross is foolishness to those who are perishing, but to us who are being saved it is the power of God. (1 Corinthians 1:18)

Charles H. Spurgeon said, "As one human mind operates upon another mind, so does the Holy Spirit influence our spirits. We are forced to use words if we would influence our fellow-men, but the Spirit of God can operate upon the human mind more directly, and communicate with it in silence. Into that matter, however, we will not dive lest we intrude where our knowledge would be drowned by our presumption."[21]

Satan, deceiving and using some men to influence us, wants to hold on to our souls by keeping us in a state of fear. But God in heaven, Who created us, has put us in a struggle with Satan for possession of our souls. God has a plan, and when we seek wisdom, we indeed do find it. In the end, God wins the souls of those who trust in Him and believe in Him. Once we believe in Him, Satan cannot have our souls. Jesus says,

"And I give them eternal life, and they shall never perish; neither shall anyone snatch them out of My hand." (Matthew 10:28)

Who shall separate us from the love of Christ?... For I am persuaded that neither death nor life, nor angels nor principalities nor powers, nor things present nor things to come, nor height nor depth, nor any other created

---

[21] *Parallel Commentary on the New Testament*, (AMG Publishers, Chattanooga, TN, 2003), pg 483

thing, shall be able to separate us from the love of God which is in Christ Jesus our Lord. (Romans 8:35a, 38–39)

God's wisdom as related to nature and our minds and souls is supernaturally linked:

He sends out His command to the earth; His word runs very swiftly. He gives snow like wool; He scatters the frost like ashes; He casts out His hail like morsels; who can stand before His cold? He sends out his word and melts them [melts the pellets of hail, which will be hundred-pound hail balls in the soon-coming Great Tribulation period: Revelation 16:21]; He causes His wind to blow, and the waters flow. (Psalm 147:16–18)

We have a powerful God. It would be wise to hear, digest, and absorb the following truthful references:

Elīhū also proceeded and said: (Job 36:1)

"Behold, God is great, and we do not know Him; nor can the number of His years be discovered. For He draws up drops of water, which distill as rain from the mist, which the clouds drop down and pour abundantly on man. Indeed, can anyone understand the spreading of clouds, the thunder from His canopy? Look, He scatters His light upon it, and covers the depths of the sea. For by these He judges the peoples; He gives food in abundance. He covers His hands with lightning, and commands it to strike. His thunder declares it, the cattle also [declare it], concerning the rising storm." (Job 36:26–33)

Ever noticed how horses and cattle grow nervous and energetic right before a storm? They indeed "declare the rising storm." Again, it's interesting that although not the first Book you see when you open the Bible, Job was written prior to Genesis, which was put together in about 1400 BC. Many scholars, as mentioned before, date the writing of Job all the way back to 2100 BC. That's four thousand years ago. No matter how old it is, the remarkable point here is that the cattle and horses have not changed.

At this also my heart trembles, and leaps from its place. Hear attentively the thunder of His voice, and the rumbling that comes from His mouth. He sends it forth under the whole heaven, His lightning to the ends of the earth. After it a voice roars; He thunders with His majestic voice, and He does not restrain them when His voice is heard. God thunders marvelously with His voice; He does great things which we cannot comprehend. For He says to the snow, "Fall on the earth"; likewise to the gentle rain and the heavy rain of His strength. He seals the hand of every man, that all men may know His work. The beasts go into dens, and remain in their lairs. From the chamber of the south comes the whirlwind [Hebrew: çûwphâh; a hurricane], and cold from the scattering winds of the north. By the breath of God ice is given, and the broad waters are frozen. Also with moisture He saturates the thick clouds; He scatters His bright clouds. And they swirl about, being turned by His guidance, that they may do whatever He commands them on the face of the whole earth. He causes it to come, whether for correction, or for His land, or for mercy. Listen to this, O Job; stand still and consider the wondrous works of God. Do you know when God dispatches them, and causes the light of His cloud to shine? Do you know how the clouds are balanced, those wondrous works of Him who is perfect in knowledge? Why are your garments hot, when He quiets the earth by the south wind? With Him, have you spread out the skies, strong as a cast metal mirror? (Job 37:1–18)

Then the LORD answered Job out of the whirlwind, and said: "Who is this who darkens counsel by words without knowledge? Now prepare yourself like a man; I will question you, and you shall answer Me. Where were you when I laid the foundations of the earth? Tell Me, if you have understanding. Who determined its measurements? Surely you know! Or who stretched the line upon it? To what were its foundations fastened? Or who laid its cornerstone, when the morning stars sang together, and all the sons of God shouted for joy? Or who shut in the sea with doors, when it burst forth and issued from the womb; when I made the clouds its garment, and thick darkness its swaddling band; when I fixed My limit for it, and set bars and doors; when I said, 'This far you may come, but no farther, and here your proud waves must stop!' Have you entered the treasury of snow, or have you seen the treasury of hail [see Revelation 16:21], which I have reserved for the time of trouble, for the day of battle and war? By what way is light diffused, or the east wind scattered over the earth? Who has divided a channel for the overflowing water, or a path for the thunderbolt, to cause it to rain on a land where there is no one, a wilderness in which there is no man; to satisfy the desolate waste, and cause to spring forth the growth of tender grass? Has the rain a father? Or who has begotten the drops of dew? From whose womb comes the ice? And the frost of heaven, who gives it birth? The waters harden like stone, and the surface of the deep is frozen. Can you bind the cluster of the Plēiadēs, or loose the belt of Orīon? Can you bring out Mazzaroth [constellations; arrangement of stars] in its season? Or can you guide the Great Bear with its cubs? Do you know the ordinances of the heavens? Can you set their dominion over the earth? Can you lift up your voice to the clouds, that an abundance of water may cover you? Can you send out lightnings, that they may go, and say to you, 'Here we are!'? Who has put wisdom in the mind? Or who has given understanding to the heart? Who can number the clouds by wisdom? Or who can pour out the bottles of heaven, when the dust hardens in clumps, and the clods cling together?" (Job 38:1–11, 22–38)

You rule the raging of the sea; when its waves rise, You still them. (Psalm 89:9)

Then He [Jesus] arose and rebuked the wind, and said to the sea, "Peace, be still!" And the wind ceased and there was a great calm. (Mark 4:39)

He has made the earth by His power, He has established the world by His wisdom, and has stretched out the heavens at His discretion. When He utters His voice, there is a multitude of waters in the heavens: and He causes the vapors to ascend from the ends of the earth. He makes lightning for the rain, He brings the wind out of His treasuries. (Jeremiah 10:12–13)

Are there any among the idols [false gods] of the nations that can cause rain? Or can the heavens give showers? Are You not He, O LORD our God? Therefore we will wait for You, since You have made all these. (Jeremiah 14:22)

Thus says the LORD, who gives the sun for a light by day, the ordinances of the moon and the stars for a light by night, who disturbs the sea, and its waves roar (the LORD of hosts is His name). (Jeremiah 31:35)

Then God said, "Let there be light"; and there was light. And God saw the light, that it was good; and God divided the light from the darkness. God called the light Day, and the darkness He called Night. So the evening and the morning were the first day. (Genesis 1:3–5)

He has made the earth by His power; He has established the world by His wisdom, and stretched out the heaven by His understanding. When He utters His voice—there is a multitude of waters in the heavens; He causes the vapors to ascend from the ends of the earth; He makes lightnings for the rain; He brings the wind out of His treasuries. (Jeremiah 51:15–16)

For He has given you the former rain faithfully, and He will cause the rain to come down for you. (Joel 2:23b)

He made the Plēiadēs and Orīon; He turns the shadow of death into morning and makes the day dark as night; He calls for the waters of the sea and pours them out on the face of the earth; The LORD is His name. (Amos 5:7–8)

That you may be sons of your Father in heaven; for He makes His sun rise on the evil and on the good, and sends rain on the just and on the unjust. (Matthew 5:45)

All things were made through Him [Jesus], and without Him nothing was made that was made. (John 1:3)

And [Paul] saying, "Men, why are you doing these things? We also are men with the same nature as you, and preach to you that you should turn from these useless things to the living God, who made the heaven, the earth, the sea, and all things that are in them, who in bygone generations allowed all nations to walk in their own ways. Nevertheless He did not leave Himself without witness, in that He did good, gave us rain from heaven and fruitful seasons, filling our hearts with food and gladness." (Acts 14:15–17)

The Father said to His Son,

"You, LORD, in the beginning laid the foundation of the earth, and the heavens are the work of Your hands." (Hebrews 1:10b)

The heavens declare the glory of God; and the firmament shows His handiwork. (Psalm 19:1; Psalms 65:9–13, 93:4, 104:13–14, 135:5–7, and 147:7–14 also declare God's glory and His mighty power.)

Because what may be known of God is manifest in them [knowledge of God is revealed to all people], for God has shown it to them. For since the creation of the world His invisible attributes are clearly seen, being understood by the things that are made, even His eternal power and Godhead [His divine nature, His deity], so that they are without excuse. (Romans 1:19–20)

It doesn't seem to be taught in science classes in schools that the earth at equinox—that is, on the first day of spring and the first day of fall—is at perfect equilibrium. When the sun is directly over the equator, the earth is not tilted toward either summer or winter; it is not wobbling, and it is in such created perfection of balance that a raw egg can be balanced on either of its pointed tips. This can only be achieved within a week either side of the first day of spring or fall. Balancing the egg requires patience, but it can be done. Why aren't kids being taught this element of miraculous creation in elementary school?

Schools and universities continue to teach the evolution of humans as being factual and the age of the earth being accurately recorded. National parks display signs explaining that the rock formations are millions of years old. However, reliable science depends upon experimentation—not unreliable methods with millions of years of differences and discrepancies, nor can we simply trust a human theory. Common sense should prevail when there is no scientific proof to rely on. These subjects have evolved to the point of indoctrinating students with man's wisdom—not God's. Repetition is called for:

It is better to trust in the LORD than to put confidence in man. (Psalm 118:8)

Trust in the LORD with all your heart, and lean not on your own understanding. (Proverbs 3:5)

But the wisdom that is from above is first pure, then peaceable, gentle, willing to yield, full of mercy and good fruits, without partiality and without hypocrisy. (James 3:17)

Chapter 4
ADMIT AND REPENT

Technological advancements have accelerated the rate of change in society. In the last thirty years, we have witnessed more development than in all of history combined. We are seeing robots that carry on conversations, automobiles capable of driving themselves, stealth aircraft, airplanes without a pilot onboard (drones), global positioning systems (GPS) that keep people from getting lost in the wilderness, smart phones, high-definition televisions, and much more. Likewise, as the population grows, people incorrectly think we have evolved into something stronger and wiser than those who lived before us.

But here is what God's Word says:

> "There is nothing new under the sun"
> (Ecclesiastes 1:10b).

Henry Ironside said, "If it is new it is not true; if it is true it is not new."

Electricity has always been here. It just took a long time for humans to harness it.

We're all unique; we're different, just like everyone else. Before going any further, it must be admitted that the author of this book is different, just like everyone else. And the writer you're reading is a sinner, just like everyone else.

For all have sinned and fall short of the glory of God.
(Romans 3:23)

Quoting Randy Amos, "When a person becomes a true believer it does not mean he is sinless. What truly happens though is that he does sin less."

It is a tremendously fearful thing for people to die with unforgiven sins, because the wrath and anger of God will be poured out on the unsaved during the Great Tribulation. But the saved people will not be subjected to such torture:

> Much more then, having now been justified [justified to be saved due to sincerely repenting] by His blood, we shall be saved from wrath through Him. (Romans 5:9)

With tremendous thanks to give to God for being saved from the eternal Lake of Fire, and with the help of the indwelling Spirit of God, believers are more readily aware that they are being tempted to offend others and to sin against God's moral commands. Upon the moment of being tempted, the Spirit reminds them to picture the cross and remember what tremendous price the Savior paid to save us. He bought us with His own blood:

> To Him who loved us and washed us from our sins in His own blood. (Revelation 1:5b)

> The church of God which He purchased with His own blood. (Acts 20:28b)

The Church that Jesus Christ purchased is not a building. The Church is the universal Church made up of all believers on the planet earth.

Eventually, when we realize we're doing something hurtful to others, when our hearts are convicted, it drives us to finally submit and admit to self—and to God—we need sound spiritual influence. Married couples need this together with each other.

When both spouses have surrendered to Christ, they are "equally yoked," and increased happiness befalls upon them. Strife can more easily develop when they are not believers or when only one spouse is a believer. In other words, they are unequally yoked, and not yoked together and not both yoked to Christ.

> Come to Me, all you who labor and are heavy laden, and I will give you rest. Take My yoke upon you and learn from Me, for I am gentle and lowly in heart, and you will find rest for your souls. For My yoke is easy and My burden is light. (Matthew 11:28–30)

In the situation where neither spouse is a believer, they could be married or, as has come to be accepted by society, common-law partners. If one suggests getting more spiritual influence into their lives, they could be blessed if they agree to try a local assembly. There was this one fairly newly wedded couple who did just that, and there was a sign posted up front of the sanctuary: "The heartbeat and passion of this church is to lead people into a life-changing relationship with Jesus Christ." Soon after giving it a try, both submitted and devoted their lives to Christ.

It's not always possible that the church can accomplish the goal of them coming to get to know God, but it can lead them in the right direction. The Word of God can inspire folks to finally buckle down and begin reading the Bible. And it's the Word of God that saves:

> So then faith comes by hearing, and hearing by the word of God. (Romans 10:17)

When reading the Ten Commandments in Exodus 20, those ten laws are what make people know about their guilt. The history of all humankind has proven that no one is capable of keeping all ten.

> For by the law is the knowledge of sin. (Romans 3:20b)

> For whoever shall keep the whole law, and yet stumble in one point, he is guilty of all. (James 2:10)

Everyone who has used God's name in vain, worshiped any other god or any idol, been dishonorable to their parents, murdered anyone, stolen anything, committed adultery, told a lie, or coveted any belongings of their neighbor is guilty.

The penalty for breaking any of these commandments is death. For example:

> The man who commits adultery with another man's wife, he who commits adultery with his neighbor's wife, the adulterer and the adulteress, shall surely be put to death. (Leviticus 20:10)

The Lord Jesus Christ took that penalty of death for all who believe in God and promises them everlasting—eternal—life in heaven. God also promises eternal suffering for those who reject Him.

Upon becoming accountable for breaking the law, everyone who does not believe is bound straight for the Lake of Fire. And the penalty for bearing false witness—that is, telling a lie—is the second death: the eternal suffering in the Lake of Fire.

All it takes to overcome and be forgiven is to sincerely repent and ask to be forgiven.

> He who overcomes shall inherit all things [heaven], and I will be his God and he shall be My son. But the cowardly, unbelieving, abominable, murderers, sexually immoral, sorcerers, idolaters, and all liars shall have their part in the lake which burns with fire and brimstone, which is the second death. (Revelation 21:7–8)

No one really wants to spend eternity suffering like that. This is not said out of anger or judgment, but with a love so strong that it persuades believers to let others know how joyful, peaceful, and wonderful it is to be forgiven.

> Then Jesus said to those Jews who believed Him, "If you abide in My word, you are My disciples indeed. And you shall know the truth, and the truth shall make you free." (John 8:31–32)

Believers are set free from the bondage of sin. In other words, we no longer live in sin—that is, practice a sinful lifestyle. If we do, then we are not truly believers because the Spirit would never indwell a practicing sinner. God separates sin from Himself.

> For such a High Priest [Jesus Christ] was fitting for us, who is holy, harmless, undefiled, separate from sinners, and has become higher than the heavens. (Hebrews 7:26)

> While he [sinful man] has uncleanness [defilement; moral blemish even in conscience] upon him, that person shall be cut off from My presence: I am the LORD. (Leviticus 22:2b)

After this temporary life on earth, God has the power to raise the dead and give eternal life. A true believer lives with this hope. It is this realization that gets people's attention, seeing that there truly is hope, and it results in changing lives, relationships, and behavior. This hope causes one to slow down and be set free from the haunting, relentless feeling of guilt.

Reading the entire Bible can seem burdensome when we look at its thickness, with all those pages. So maybe it's better to start somewhere other than "In the beginning." The Gospel of John is a good starting point. All the Gospel Books—Matthew, Mark, Luke, and John—are good, and eventually, that last part, the Book of the Revelation of Jesus Christ, is an attention getter: That Book is the last Book in the Bible, and it's speaking about what happens at the beginning of the end and near the end of time for this earth. It can be a shock when reading this last part of Scripture, but it is quite mellow compared to what the shock will be for people who must bow the knee to the just God at the Great White Throne and face the consequence for having not accepted Him as Savior.

> Therefore God also has highly exalted Him [Jesus] and given Him the name which is above every name, that at the name of Jesus every knee should bow, of those in heaven, and of those on earth, and of those under the earth, and that every tongue should confess that Jesus Christ is Lord, to the glory of God the Father. (Philippians 2:9–11)

When one honestly asks the question of one self, "Have I ever told a lie?" the answer is invariably affirmative. Of course, telling lies isn't the only thing we've done to offend God or to hurt others whom He created. Part of that passage in Revelation 21:8 states that the sexually immoral would also have their part in the Lake of Fire. This is when we learn we are in trouble: We'd be suffering for our eternal future. We need God's help. We all need the Savior.

The saving grace is found in the One who took the penalty for us, and we find our hope for being resurrected back to life from what would be our first and only death. God raised Jesus from the dead back to life on the third day. This is definitely worth repeating:

> And God both raised up the Lord and will also raise us up by His power. (1 Corinthians 6:14)

> Knowing that He who raised up the Lord Jesus will also raise us up with Jesus, and will present us with you. (2 Corinthians 4:14)

> But if the Spirit of Him who raised Jesus from the dead dwells in you, He who raised Christ from the dead will also give life to your mortal bodies through His Spirit who dwells in you. (Romans 8:11)

For all who believe in Him, God promises to also raise us back to eternal life.

> And this is the promise that He has promised us— eternal life. (1 John 2:25)

God even promises to give us a new glorious body:

> For our citizenship is in heaven, from which we also eagerly wait for the Savior, the Lord Jesus Christ, who will transform our lowly body that it may be conformed to His glorious body, according to the working by which He is able even to subdue all things to Himself. (Philippians 3:20–21)

That is called hope.

Wisdom requires learning. There are at least four Rs of learning. These are

1. Read
2. Repetition (repeat, refresh, or review)
3. Recall (recite or remember)
4. Recency

You, the reader, have probably noticed some repetition. Considering wisdom, for us to be well prepared for our eternal futures, we need to have God's Word recent and fresh on our hearts and in our minds. It is vitally important to regularly read God's Word each day, to remember what the Savior did for all of us sinners. Appropriate repetition will continue as we consider wisdom.

Who Is God?

It can be confusing to discuss who God is. But at last, and thankfully so, we can try to find out. There are so many teachings in this world about who God is compared to who He isn't. Many people find out who God isn't before finding out who He is. God is truth. God is three Persons: Father, Son, and Holy Spirit. Without any One of the Three, then the god being mulled over is not the truth. Jesus said,

> "I am the way, the truth, and the life. No one comes to the Father except through Me" (John 14:6b).

It has been said, "The only thing we learn from history is that we learn nothing from history." Without truth, the whole value of history becomes extinct. Revising history is senseless. For the study of history to be meaningful and worthwhile, we must maintain truth.

There is a big difference between wisdom and knowledge. We can have knowledge of many, many things. We can learn from books that the earth is billions of years old, that we evolved from primates, that we can control the weather, and on and on. But the difference between knowledge and wisdom is this:

Knowledge: We can know all things that are taught to us if we listen to what is said or are educated with what is written.

Wisdom: Having wisdom is to understand what is true and what isn't about all the things we know.

When knowledge goes beyond the truth, it does not surpass wisdom.

Knowledge makes a positive impact only when it's within the realm of wisdom. True wisdom always remains within the realm of truth. Truth does not fail.

Noah Webster's 1828 *American Dictionary of the English Language* gives this definition of wisdom: "The right use or exercise of knowledge; the choice of laudable ends, and of the best means to accomplish them. This is wisdom in *act, effect*, and *practice*. If wisdom is to be considered as a *faculty* of the mind, it is the faculty of discerning or judging what is most just, proper and useful, and if it is to be considered as an *acquirement*, it is the knowledge and use of what is best, most just, most proper, most conducive to prosperity or happiness."[22]

The benefit of having wisdom and being able to discern and understand God's Word comes only by one's belief and therefore having received the indwelling Spirit of God:

---

[22] The original *American Dictionary of the English Language*, Noah Webster, 1828, s.v. "wisdom"

But the natural man [the person who does not believe in God] does not receive the things of the Spirit of God, for they [the Words of God] are foolishness to him [the natural man]; nor can he know them [the Words of God], because they are spiritually discerned. (1 Corinthians 2:14)

According to the same dictionary, "Philosophy is the love of wisdom."[23] In the period of time between the Old and New Testaments, Greek culture introduced several famous philosophers.

Alexander the Great, in many respects the greatest conqueror of all time, was the central figure of this brief period. He conquered Persia, Babylon, Palestine, Syria, Egypt, and western India. Although he died at the age of thirty-three, having reigned over Greece only thirteen years, his influence lived long after him.... Under his influence the world began to speak and study the Greek language. This process, called Hellenization, included the adoption of Greek culture and religion in all parts of the world.[24]

That Greek culture introduced philosophers like Socrates and Plato. Some scholars claim the Greek philosophers determined the earth was round as far back as the sixth century BC, long before Christopher Columbus sailed to the New World. However, God's Word still makes fools of them because of the God-given inspiration for Isaiah in about 700 BC:

Have you not known? Have you not heard? Has it not been told you from the beginning? Have you not understood from the foundations of the earth? It is He who sits above the circle of the earth, and its inhabitants

---

[23] The original *American Dictionary of the English Language*, Noah Webster, 1828, s.v. "philosophy"

[24] *Believer's Bible Commentary*, William MacDonald, (Thomas Nelson, 1995), "The Intertestamental Period," "The Greek Era (336–323 BC), pg 1186

are like grasshoppers, who stretches out the heavens like a curtain, and spreads them out like a tent to dwell in. (Isaiah 40:21–22)

Like being the Source of wisdom, the Source of discernment is also God Himself. He knows our every thought and action.

For the word of God [the Bible—all Scripture] is living and powerful, and sharper than any two-edged sword, piercing even to the division of soul and spirit, and of joints and marrow, and is a discerner of the thoughts and intents of the heart. (Hebrews 4:12)

To be wise is to consider wisdom and discernment in all the decisions we make every moment every day. We need to make the best possible choices for the following reason:

"For God [the Father] gave His only begotten Son, that whoever believes in Him should not perish but have everlasting life" (John 3:16).

Like wisdom and knowledge, knowledge and belief are also different: We can know what the Bible says without actually believing what it says. Knowing does not require believing. Belief occurs only when our hearts and minds are fully convinced, totally persuaded that what we know is actually true.

The importance of eternity cannot possibly be overemphasized. Lacking wisdom can result in conscious, eternal suffering in the Lake of Fire, which will never be quenched.

We need to swallow our pride, stop rejecting the Lord Jesus Christ, and repent.

The first time He is quoted in the Gospel according to Mark, Jesus says,

"The time is fulfilled, and the kingdom of God is at hand. Repent and believe in the gospel" (Mark 1:15b).

ADMIT AND REPENT

The word *repent* means,

> And do not be conformed to this world, but be
> transformed by the renewing of your mind
> (Romans 12:2a)

In other words, to repent means to have a change of mind and a change of heart, to be sincerely remorseful for having offended. It means to stop going the way of the world—man's way—and turn around and go toward God—the Lord's way. The rest of the verse goes on,

> that you may prove what is that good and acceptable and
> perfect will of God. (Romans 12:2b).

This does not mean that we do those good and acceptable things to save ourselves. We cannot do anything to save ourselves. Only, and simply, by believing in God, having faith in Him, can we be saved. The *Choice Gleanings Calendar* for April 15, 2019, quotes an Old Testament prophet who told us we cannot buy our way to heaven:

> Neither their silver nor their gold shall be able to deliver
> them in the day of the LORD's wrath. (Zephaniah 1:18)

Carl Knott issues the following commentary: "Forgiveness cannot be bought. Money is the universal passport to everywhere except heaven. But the gospel goes out even to him *'that hath no money'* (Isaiah 55:1b KJV). Nor are spiritual life, power, or positions in the church for sale....

> But Peter said to him [the sorcerer] "Your money perish
> with you, because you thought that the gift of God could
> be purchased with money!" (Acts 8:20).

Some say that money makes the world go round, but God is neither swayed by them nor their money."

The price for our way to heaven was paid by Jesus when He took the punishment that we deserved. He didn't deserve to be punished, because

He is sinless. There is no sin in Him. We're the ones who committed all the offenses, from using God's name in a blaspheming way to telling lies, and everything in between. No, we cannot buy our way into heaven, nor can we do any good deeds to get there. The only things we can do are repent and believe. Not even going to the church meeting, or getting water baptized, or helping a little old lady across the street, or anything else can get us to heaven. God's Word reminds us that if we think being good enough will get us to heaven, then we are boasting that we do not need the Savior, that we are so good we can save ourselves. If we don't need the Savior, then He died needlessly. Here's what God's Word says:

Where is boasting then? It is excluded. (Romans 3:27a)

For by grace you have been saved through faith, and that not of yourselves; it is the gift of God, and not of works, lest anyone should boast. (Ephesians 2:8–9)

I do not set aside the grace of God; for if righteousness comes through the law [supposedly being able to obey all the commandments], then Christ died in vain. (Galatians 2:21)

The Lord Jesus Christ died for nothing if, in fact, we could have been able to save ourselves. But let's face it; no one has ever kept all those commandments, except for the sinless Son of God.

For there is not a just man on earth who does good and does not sin. (Ecclesiastes 7:20)

There is none righteous; no, not one. (Romans 3:10b)

Only the Lord Jesus Christ, when He was on this earth as Man, was able to keep all the commandments:

For He [the Father] made Him [the Son] who knew no sin to be sin for us, that we might become the righteousness of God in Him. (2 Corinthians 5:21)

Who committed no sin, nor was deceit found in His mouth. (1 Peter 2:22)

And you know that He was manifested [revealed] to take away our sins, and in Him there is no sin. (1 John 3:5)

How much more shall the blood of Christ, who through the eternal Spirit offered Himself without spot [without blemish; without sin] to God, cleanse your conscience from dead works to serve the living God? (Hebrews 9:14)

Of course, there are lots of wonderful people here on earth who sincerely try to be good. But being honest with integrity for God and self, all would admit they slip and stumble every now and then. If all the believers who are good people go to heaven just because they are good, then they have it made—along with unbelieving people. However, if good unbelievers consider wisdom, they would understand that the believer just might be right in that we are saved only by grace, not by our works, good deeds, or obedience. Jesus Christ already did the work—on the cross. What an important decision: whether to surrender and accept Jesus Christ as the only way, a decision that has eternal consequences. Again, our God, Creator, and Savior is quoted, this time with the emphasis on the word *life*:

I am the way, the truth, and the life. No one comes to the Father except through Me. (John 14:6b)

Without exception, the most important decision people can make during this temporary life on earth is to believe in God, to repent, and to accept the Lord Jesus Christ as their one and only Savior and the only way to the Father in heaven. Believing in God is knowing that God is three Persons: the Father, the Son of God Jesus, and the Holy Spirit:

Whoever denies the Son does not have the Father either; he who acknowledges the Son has the Father also. (1 John 2:23)

Why is Jesus called the Son of God? It is because it is the Holy Spirit Who caused Mary to bear Him:

> That which is conceived [begotten] in her is of the Holy Spirit. (Matthew 1:20b)

> The Holy Spirit will come upon you, and the power of the Highest will overshadow you; therefore, also, that Holy One who is to be born will be called the Son of God. (Luke 1:35b)

The Son of God was fully Man while also being fully God. The Father sent Him down from heaven. He existed for all eternity past, still exists, and always will exist for all eternity.

> Jesus Christ is the same yesterday, today, and forever. (Hebrews 13:8)

> In the beginning was the Word, and the Word was with God, and the Word was God. (John 1:1)

> And the Word became flesh and dwelt among us. (John 1:14a)

While Jesus Christ is His only begotten Son, our God and Father sincerely desires us to be His adopted children. All who truly believe in God and His Gospel message are the Father's adopted children.

We are saved from His wrath and become His children by grace. Grace is something we receive but do not deserve. G-R-A-C-E = God's Riches At Christ's Expense. A salesman cannot sell this grace to anyone as a ticket to heaven. Salvation is free for only those who believe in God. It is not for sale. On the cross, Christ already paid the tremendous price.

> But the free gift which came from many offenses resulted in justification. (Romans 5:16b)

As the Father wants us to be His children, God, the only begotten Son, loves us and calls us His brethren—that is, His brothers and sisters:

> For both He who sanctifies [sets apart from the world] and those who are being sanctified are all of one, for which reason He is not ashamed to call them brethren. (Hebrews 2:11)

> For this is good and acceptable in the sight of God our Savior, who desires all men to be saved and to come to the knowledge of the truth. (1 Timothy 2:3–4)

The New World Translation—not the Holy Bible—is the key writing for the Jehovah's Witnesses. In 1879, they began changing the Holy Bible to deceive seekers of Almighty God into thinking that Jesus Christ is not equal to the Father as a Person of God.

> Who is a liar but he who denies that Jesus is the Christ? He is antichrist who denies the Father and the Son. Whoever denies the Son does not have the Father either; he who acknowledges the Son has the Father also. (1 John 2:22–23)

The Lord Jesus says,

> "For assuredly, I say to you, till heaven and earth pass away, one jot [Hebrew: the smallest letter] or one tittle [the smallest stroke in a Hebrew letter], will by no means pass from the law till all is fulfilled" (Matthew 5:18).

Jehovah's Witnesses, supposedly being good, peddle pamphlets door-to-door in many American towns and cities. They believe they can work their way to heaven. Actually, they do not believe in heaven in the way the Bible explains it. Rather, they believe they will stay on earth (this earth, which the Bible tells us will be destroyed).

> The elements will melt with fervent heat; both the earth and the works that are in it will be burned up. (2 Peter 3:10)

Eighteen hundred years before the Jehovah's Witnesses were founded, John the apostle, led and inspired by the Spirit, described them perfectly:

> For many deceivers have gone out into the world who do not confess Jesus Christ as coming in the flesh. This is a deceiver and an antichrist. Look to yourselves, that we do not lose those things we worked for, but that we may receive a full reward. Whoever transgresses and does not abide in the doctrine of Christ does not have God. He who abides in the doctrine of Christ has both the Father and the Son. If anyone comes to you and does not bring this doctrine, do not receive him into your house and greet him; for he who greets him shares in his evil deeds. (2 John 7–11)

The New World Translation of the Jehovah's Witnesses has taken away many truths from the Holy Bible.

The fourth Book in the New Testament of the Bible, the Gospel according to John, for example, says this:

> "In the beginning was the Word, and the Word was with God, and the Word was God" (John 1:1).

The New World Translation changed the same verse to say this: "In the beginning was the Word and the Word was with God, and the Word was *a god*" (emphasis added).

Their insistence upon declaring that the Lord Jesus Christ is not Almighty God contradicts eight verses in the last Book of the Bible—the Revelation of Jesus Christ—which verify that Jesus Christ is indeed Almighty God. This is not the only place in the Scriptures that confirms Jesus is, in fact, Jehovah God. For example, the Lord God Jesus says,

> "I am the Alpha and the Omega, the Beginning and the End," says the Lord, "who is and who was and who is to come, the Almighty" (Revelation 1:8).

The Second Person of God—known by name as Jesus after the Father sent Him—is the only Person of God Who has ever appeared to humans.

> Not that anyone has seen the Father, except He who is from God [the Son of God]; He has seen the Father (John 6:46)

Jesus appeared in the time of the New Testament, and He appeared—not as "Jesus" yet—in the Old Testament. He appeared many times. Here is but one example:

> Then the Jews said to Him, "You are not yet fifty years old, and have You seen Abraham?" Jesus said to them, "Most assuredly I say to you, before Abraham was I AM." (John 8:57–58)

The Old Testament confirms what Jesus said. When God told Moses to go and speak to the Israelites, Moses responded by asking Jehovah God Almighty how to give the name of God to the Israelites:

> Then Moses said to God, "Indeed, when I come to the children of Israel and say to them, 'The God of your fathers has sent me to you,' and they say to me, 'What is His name?' what shall I say to them?" And God said to Moses, "I AM WHO I AM." And He said, "Thus you shall say to the children of Israel, 'I AM has sent me to you.'" (Exodus 3:13–14)

> And God spoke to Moses and said to him: "I am the LORD. I appeared to Abraham, to Isaac, and to Jacob, as God Almighty, but by My name LORD [Hebrew: YHWH, traditionally Jehovah] I was not known to them." (Exodus 6:2–3)

When Jesus was taken prisoner and spoke to the ones who came to capture Him:

Now when He said to them, "I am He," they drew back and fell to the ground. (John 18:6)

Earlier, the Lord Jesus was answering the Jews, who were looking for a reason to kill Him, and after a thorough explanation of their mistake in rejecting Him, Jesus ended with this:

> "For if you believed Moses, you would believe Me; for he wrote about Me. But if you do not believe his writings; how will you believe My words?" (John 5:46–47)

The Bible warns us four times not to add to it nor take away from it. We're not to change the contents. The Jehovah's Witnesses need to be reading and heeding this:

> For I testify to everyone who hears the words of the prophecy of this book: If anyone adds to these things, God will add to him the plagues that are written in this book; and if anyone takes away from the words of the book of this prophecy, God shall take away his part from the Book of Life, from the holy city, and from the things which are written in this book.
> (Revelation 22:18–19)

Other verses warn us not to attempt to change God's Word: Deuteronomy 4:2, 12:32; Joshua 1:7; Proverbs 30:5–6; Ecclesiastes 3:14; Matthew 5:18.

The fact that Jesus Christ is Almighty God with the Father and the Holy Spirit is not being pointed out here to degrade the people who are Jehovah's Witnesses. Indeed,

> "God our Savior desires all men to be saved and come to the knowledge of the truth" (1 Timothy 2:3b–4).

What is being refuted is the false teaching that has indoctrinated some wonderful people (whom God created, loves, and desires to save).

True believers in God are also indoctrinated, but with the sound doctrine of the Holy Bible.

> But we know that the law is good if one uses it lawfully, knowing this: that the law is not made for a righteous person, but for the lawless and insubordinate, for the ungodly and for sinners,... and if there is any other thing that is contrary to sound doctrine. (1 Timothy 1:8–9a, 10b)

> For the time will come when they will not endure sound doctrine, but according to their own desires, because they have itching ears, they will heap up for themselves teachers; and they will turn their ears away from the truth, and be turned aside to fables. (2 Timothy 4:3–4)

> Holding fast the faithful word as he has been taught, that he may be able, by sound doctrine, both to exhort [encourage] and convict those who contradict. (Titus 1:9)

> But as for you, speak the things which are proper for sound doctrine. (Titus 2:1)

Jehovah's Witnesses are not the only ones who stray from the sound teaching of God's Word; the Lord loves the Muslim people too. And believers share God's desire for all to be saved. True Christians share His love for them. Although some followers of Islam are extreme terrorists, Jesus Christ teaches us to love our enemies:

> But I say to you who hear: Love your enemies, do good to those who hate you. (Luke 6:27)

The Qur'an, the key writing of Islam, was written by men who attempted to recall what Muhammad had said, long after Muhammad had died. Furthermore, Muhammad spoke to them approximately six hundred years after the Lord Jesus was crucified and resurrected back to life from the dead. The Qur'an writings include parts of the Holy Bible that were changed to suit the needs of the false Islamic teaching.

Three huge differences between Christianity and Islam are striking right away: First, the Lord Jesus Christ was raised back to life and seen by over five hundred witnesses for forty days, and He was seen ascending back upward to heaven. He is still living and promises to return. But Muhammad's body is still decaying in the grave.

Second, the Qur'an teaches that fatherhood cannot be associated with Allah. This should certainly influence one's spiritual way of reasoning. How could Allah possibly be the Father of the Son of God—that is, the Lord Jesus—if Allah has nothing to do with fatherhood? The realization that God and Allah are two entirely different entities confirms the fact that there could only be one conclusive, absolute truth.

Third, the Qur'an has many contradictions, in stark contrast to the Holy Bible. The Bible is also referred to as God's Word or the Scriptures, in which there are no contradictions. The Word of God is pure and flawless (Psalm 12:6; Proverbs 30:5). People who thinks they found a contradiction need to compare Scripture to Scripture and keep the entire Scripture in context. Text without context is pretext.

The Qur'an stating that Allah does not have the attribute of fatherhood is not the only severe difference from Christianity. It also tremendously demeans the divinity of the Lord Jesus Christ by saying that Jesus is simply one of over 124,000 prophets sent by Allah. The Sunni and Shi'a sects teach that a family member of Muhammad is still alive and will appear with Jesus when He returns. But God's Word says this:

> He [Jesus] humbled Himself and became obedient to the point of death, even the death of the cross. Therefore God also has highly exalted Him and given Him the name which is above every name, that at the name of Jesus every knee should bow, of those in heaven, and of those on earth, and of those under the earth, and that every tongue should confess that Jesus Christ is Lord, to the glory of God the Father. (Philippians 2:8b–11)

No wonder that when some people get upset to the maximum, they break the Third Commandment by using the most powerful name in the entire created universe (before I was saved, I was guilty of that one too). They take the name of the Lord our God in vain, the name "Jesus Christ." If a man accidentally hits his thumb with a hammer, we never hear him shout, "Oh, Buddha!" or "Oh, Brahma cow!" or "Oh, Allah!" or any other false god. Instead, they shout the name which is above every name—Jesus Christ.

> Therefore God also has highly exalted Him and given Him the name which is above every name, that at the name of Jesus every knee should bow.
> (Philippians 2:9–10a)

Chapter 5

IN PURSUIT OF WISDOM

In an air force leadership school we were taught the following trait: "The first step for a new leader is to gain the respect of his people, and the second step is to maintain their respect. When speaking in front of your subordinates, if you use God's name for no good reason, or if you use foul language, some of your subordinates might think it's cute or tough, but some might be offended by it. You will not gain any respect for using offensive speech, and you certainly will not lose any respect if you don't speak such."

In pursuing wisdom, the first step is to have reverence or fear of the Lord, and the second step is to sincerely seek Him:

> I love those who love me, and those who seek me diligently will find me. (Proverbs 8:17)

> And you will seek Me and find Me, when you search for Me with all your heart. (Jeremiah 29:13)

Jesus said,

> "So I say to you, ask, and it will be given to you; seek, and you will find; knock, and it will be opened to you" (Luke 11:9).

> Every word of God is pure; He is a shield to those who put their trust in Him. (Proverbs 30:5)

> The words of the LORD are pure words, like silver tried in a furnace of earth, purified seven times. (Psalm 12:6)

> As for God, His way is perfect; the word of the LORD is proven; He is a shield to all who trust in Him. (Psalm 18:30)

The Bible is a library consisting of sixty-six Books that were written over a period of about sixteen hundred years by over forty writers, and miraculously, the Bible is in agreement with itself. There are no errors or contradictions. Of course, if the Bible is not read in depth, and not read by comparing Scripture to Scripture, and not kept in correct context, some will say there are contradictions. But if the Bible is diligently read with honesty and integrity, and kept in context, it is absolutely flawless. This is only possible because of the fact that God Himself is the Author, not the writer. The Author who inspired the writers had Paul write this to Timothy:

> All Scripture is given by inspiration of God (2 Timothy 3:16a).

And God the Author inspired Peter to include this:

> knowing this first, that no prophecy of Scripture is of any private interpretation, for prophecy never came by the will of man, but holy men of God spoke as they were moved by the Holy Spirit (2 Peter 1:20–21).

> God cannot lie. (Titus 1:2b)

> The word of God is living. (Hebrews 4:12)

> The word of the LORD endures forever. (Isaiah 40:8 and 1 Peter 1:25)

Some calculate there to be over three hundred messianic prophecies in the Hebrew Scriptures (the Old Testament). The astounding mathematical impossibility of someone fulfilling these prophecies is mind-blowing (see our booklet, "Scientific Facts in the Bible" for more). The scientific probability that any one person could fulfill just eight specific prophecies is 1 in 10 to the 17th power. If we took that number of silver dollars (1,000,000,000,000,000,000), drew a black X on only one (of those silver dollars), they would cover the entire state of Texas two feet deep. Now blindfold a man and tell him to travel as far as he wishes and then pick up only one silver dollar, and it must be the marked one. What chance would he have of picking up the right one? It would be exactly the same odds that just eight of the messianic prophecies would all come true in any one person—yet they all (all three hundred) came true in Christ (adapted from *Science Speaks* by Peter Stoner).[25]

The Bible warns us more than sixty-five times to "watch out," "be careful," or "to not be deceived." In the postmodern church age, we can find many mega-churches and prosperity-preaching churches. The Scriptures are clear:

> Enter by the narrow gate; for wide is the gate and broad is the way that leads to destruction, and there are many who go in by it. Because narrow is the gate and difficult is the way which leads to life, and there are few who find it. (Matthew 7:13–14)

> For thus says the Lord GOD: "The city that goes out by a thousand shall have a hundred left, and that which goes out by a hundred shall have ten left" (Amos 5:3a)

> "Seek Me and live" (Amos 5:4b)

God is not as interested in big numbers of followers as He is in their hearts—their sincere pursuit of Him. God Himself puts it this way:

25 Living Waters website, "Astounding Prophecies That Persuade People to Believe", Allen Atzbi, July 2, 2018, 2nd and 8th paragraph (June 2019) https://www.livingwaters.com/astounding-prophecies-that-persuade-people-to-believe/

> For I desire mercy and not sacrifice, and the knowledge
> of God more than burnt offerings. (Hosea 6:6)

We read that only a few find the gate that leads to life. The Scriptures mention the "remnant" ninety-two times. What's the meaning of *remnant*? The 1828 Noah Webster dictionary gives this: "Remnant: 1. Residue; that which is left after the separation, removal or destruction of a part." This 190-year-old dictionary even includes this: "The *remnant* that are left of the captivity" (Nehemiah 1). Here is that verse:

> And they said to me, "The survivors [KJV: remnant]
> who are left from the captivity in the province are there
> in great distress and reproach." (Nehemiah 1:3a)

Nehemiah goes on to say,

> So I came to Jerusalem and was there three days. Then
> I arose in the night, I and a few men with me
> (Nehemiah 2:11–12a).

Just like Noah and his family of eight, there were only a few who were saved. Time and resources were lacking, and their number was small, but they built that wall. The things that happened to the many Israelites who did not yet make it back to Jerusalem, and all the other Israelites who did not survive in the Old Testament, are explained in the New Testament, which tells us these things occurred for our learning. The Church Age, which began nearly two thousand years ago at Pentecost, is the last age before the beginning of the end.

> Now all these things happened to them as examples,
> and they were written for our admonition [instruction],
> upon whom the ends of the ages have come.
> (1 Corinthians 10:11)

> Though the number of the children of Israel be as the
> sand of the sea, the remnant will be saved.
> (Romans 9:27b, quoting Isaiah 10:22)

> For thus says the LORD GOD: "The city that goes out by a thousand shall have a hundred left, and that which goes out by a hundred shall have ten left to the house of Israel." (Amos 5:3)

> There is a way that seems right to a man, but its end is the way of death. (Proverbs 16:25)

When we think of the wide gate that leads to destruction and the huge, mega number of lost souls, we are so very privileged and blessed to be a part of the remnant to which God has given life. We thank Him for giving us discernment and wisdom to overcome Satan's evil corruption. We pray for all those who seek what the world has to offer, instead of seeking God our Savior, so that they may be transformed by the renewing of their minds.

Reasoning informs us that the larger number of Jews who were exiled and not allowed to remain in the Promised Land suffered because they were rebellious. They renounced the authority and dominion of Almighty God, to whom we all owe allegiance due to Him being our Creator and Savior.

The Book of Ezekiel was written while the Jews were being exiled to Babylon from Jerusalem and Judea. The word *rebellious,* seen seventeen times in Ezekiel alone, describes the way the people were behaving in favor of false prophets (or false teachers, in today's cultures) but were against genuine prophets. Their rebellion was the reason they did not receive the grace and mercy of God. People today who've heard the Gospel message and know about Jesus Christ but still reject Him are being rebellious.

The prosperity preachers need to read and heed the following:

> Then Jesus said to His disciples, "Assuredly, I say to you that it is hard for a rich man to enter the kingdom of heaven." (Matthew 19:23)

And the disciples were astonished at His words. But Jesus answered again and said to them, "Children, how hard it is for those who trust in riches to enter the kingdom of God!" (Mark 10:24)

Now a certain ruler asked Him, saying, "Good Teacher, what shall I do to inherit eternal life?... And when Jesus saw that he became very sorrowful, He said, "How hard it is for those who have riches to enter the kingdom of God!" (Luke 18:18, 25)

Now the Pharisees, who were lovers of money, also heard all these things, and they derided Him. (Luke 16:14)

[If anyone is obsessed with] useless wranglings [constant friction] of men of corrupt minds and destitute of the truth, who suppose that godliness is a means of gain. From such withdraw yourself. Now godliness with contentment is great gain. For we brought nothing into this world, and it is certain we can carry nothing out. And having food and clothing, with these we shall be content. But those who desire to be rich fall into temptation and a snare, and into many foolish and harmful lusts which drown men in destruction and perdition. For the love of money is a root of all kinds of evil, for which some have strayed from the faith in their greediness, and pierced themselves through with many sorrows. (1 Timothy 6:3a, 4b, 5–10)

One of many prosperity preachers exposed by Justin Peters was captured on DVD[26] preaching to his television audience about how they would prosper if they would listen for how Isaiah 54:17 speaks of prospering. Then he excitedly told them to send in their $54.17 right now. Apparently, he'd found the word *prosper* in Isaiah 54:17 but either did not know

---

[26]   *Clouds without Water* DVD (Justin Peters Ministries, 2016), (June 2019) https://justinpeters.org/product/clouds-without-water-ii/

what it meant or else figured no one would go to the trouble to look it up. The verse is actually quoting the LORD assuring the Israelites that their enemies would not prosper. It does not tell the Israelites that they themselves will prosper monetarily:

> "No weapon formed against you shall prosper, and every tongue which rises against you in judgment you shall condemn. This is the heritage of the servants of the LORD, and their righteousness is from Me," says the LORD. (Isaiah 54:17)

What both the preacher and his listeners really need to hear is this:

> They have forsaken the right way and gone astray, following the way of Bālaam the son of Bēor, who loved the wages of unrighteousness. (2 Peter 2:15)

And this:

> Woe to them! For they have… run greedily in the error of Bālaam for profit. (Jude 11a, c)

We need to use discernment when listening to or reading human doctrine, even for what we see on television or read in newspapers or magazines. *National Geographic* magazine on November 25, 2016, titled "Jesus and the Origins of Christianity," depicted an artist's rendition of the Man, Jesus Christ, on the cover.[27] The theme for that periodical was "The Life of Jesus Christ." The urging to be careful, watch out, and to not be deceived was plainly justified not only inside on the first page, but also in the very first sentence. It falsely stated, "Jesus was born in Lower Galilee." No, Jesus was not born in Galilee, but in Bethlehem of Judah. It would be wise to listen to the words in annual Christmas hymns, like "O Little Town of Bethlehem" or "O Come All Ye Faithful" ("Come ye to Bethlehem") or "Hark, the Herald Angels Sing" ("Christ is born in

---

[27] Jesus and the Origins of Christianity, National Geographic (Single Issue Magazine, November 25, 2016), (June 2019), https://www.amazon.com/National-Geographic-Jesus-Origins-Christianity/dp/1683306775

Bethlehem") and more. But better yet, consider where the hymn writers got the wisdom from:

> But you, Bethlehem Ephrathah, though you are little among the thousands of Judah, yet out of you shall come forth to Me the One to be Ruler in Israel, whose goings forth are from of old, from everlasting.
> (Micah 5:2, written in about 700 BC)

> Now after Jesus was born in Bethlehem of Judea in the days of Herod the king. (Matthew 2:1a)

> Joseph also went up from Galilee, out of the city of Nazareth, into Judea, to the city of David, which is called Bethlehem, because he was of the house and lineage of David, to be registered with Mary, his betrothed wife, who was with child. So it was, that while they were there, the days were completed for her to be delivered. And she brought forth her firstborn Son, and wrapped Him in swaddling cloths, and laid Him in a manger, because there was no room for them in the inn. (Luke 2:4–7)

The editor and writers of *National Geographic* should have prayed and done more thorough research, to seek sound doctrine diligently with a sincere heart. God is serious about not changing anything about Him or what He says.

> For I am the LORD, I do not change. (Malachi 3:6)

Pursuing wisdom prompts clarification: The Bible teaches that the one Almighty God is Triune: one God in three Persons. The three Persons are the Father, the Son, and the Holy Spirit. The Lord Jesus Christ is Almighty God, just as the Father and the Holy Spirit are Persons of Almighty God.

The term *Trinity* does not appear in Scripture; it is an acceptable theological term we use to define God as the true, undivided unity expressed in His threefold nature: God the Father, God the Son, and God the Holy Spirit. Almighty God is a divine mystery beyond human comprehension.

Only through scriptural consideration and revelation can we even begin to reflect upon the three Persons of God. By reading and staying in the Word, we can begin to understand the dynamic character of God and note that He is real and not some philosophical or religious speculation or any kind of being that comes from our imagination. We learn that the Three are not three separate gods, and we do not focus solely on the aspect of God the Father being the only one who is God. The essence of God's nature demands the understanding that it is essential to include all Three. The Three of Them are God—God Almighty. God the Son and the Holy Spirit are not placed in lower categories and made any less divine.

> Let this mind be in you which was also in Christ Jesus, who, being in the form of God, did not consider it robbery to be equal with God, but made Himself of no reputation, taking the form of a bondservant, and coming in the likeness of men. And being found in appearance as a man, He humbled Himself and became obedient to the point of death, even the death of the cross. Therefore God also has highly exalted Him and given Him the name which is above every name, that at the name of Jesus every knee should bow, of those in heaven, and of those on earth, and of those under the earth, and that every tongue should confess that Jesus Christ is Lord, to the glory of God the Father. (Philippians 2:5–11)

Seeking Wisdom

The Source of wisdom is our very Creator. Wisdom does not just happen. We must seek wisdom.

> I love those who love me, and those who seek me diligently will find me. (Proverbs 8:17)

For I know the thoughts that I think toward you, says the LORD, thoughts of peace and not of evil, to give you a future and a hope. Then you will call upon Me and go and pray to Me, and I will listen to you. And you will seek Me and find Me, when you search for Me with all your heart. (Jeremiah 29:11–13)

Ask and it will be given to you, seek, and you will find; knock, and it will be opened to you. For everyone who asks receives, and he who seeks finds, and to him who knocks it will be opened. (Matthew 7:7–8)

If any of you lacks wisdom, let him ask of God, who gives to all liberally and without reproach, and it will be given to him. But let him ask in faith, with no doubting, for he who doubts is like a wave of the sea driven and tossed by the wind. (James 1:5–6)

True believers often times do pray for wisdom, and it results in motivation to dig deeper into the Scriptures. Since God is the Source of wisdom and the one who inspired every word in the Bible, then wisdom prayed for is wisdom given. The wisdom is gained from God through His prescriptions provided by Himself. God is blessed by the believer who reads, absorbs, digests, and applies those remedies to others. After all, the believer who has been cured from a sin condition is prompted to help others in need.

The Book of Proverbs could be called the *book of wisdom*. The first nine chapters are jam-packed with wisdom herself. Notice the gender of that pronoun. In Latin-based languages, there are genders assigned to nouns. For example, in French, the moon is feminine, and the sun is masculine. However, in German, it is the opposite: the moon is masculine, and the sun is feminine. The Hebrew language, like Latin languages, also assigns gender to nouns. So wisdom, in the original Old Testament Hebrew language, is a feminine noun. In the New Testament, the Greek language renders the word *church* a feminine name. The first stanza in the first verse of the hymn "The Church's One Foundation" goes like this: "The church's one foundation is Jesus Christ *her* Lord." Proverbs chapter 8 has wisdom pleading with us to listen. It begins like this:

> Does not wisdom cry out, and understanding lift up her voice? She takes her stand on the top of the high hill, beside the way, where the paths meet. She cries out by the gates, at the entry of the city, at the entrance of the doors: "To you, O men, I call, and my voice is to the sons of men. O you simple ones, understand prudence, and you fools, be of an understanding heart. Listen, for I will speak of excellent things, and from the opening of my lips will come right things; for my mouth will speak truth; wickedness is an abomination to my lips, All the words of my mouth are with righteousness; nothing crooked or perverse is in them. They are all plain to him who understands, and right to those who find knowledge. Receive my instruction, and not silver, and knowledge rather than choice gold; for wisdom is better than rubies, and all the things one may desire cannot be compared with her. (Proverbs 8:1–11)

Wisdom comes from our Creator. Who is our Creator?

> The LORD by wisdom founded the earth; by understanding He established the heavens; by His knowledge the depths were broken up, and clouds drop down the dew. (Proverbs 3:19–20)

It goes without saying that to understand Who God is can be confusing, especially with our multiple inputs for numerous gods. How could you possibly prove that the God you believe in is any better than the one someone else believes in? Only by the constant guidance you receive from the true God can you prove your personal God even to yourself. Once you accept the one true Triune God, you realize the change that has taken place in your life. As a Christian, you would answer, "I've been led to a life-changing relationship with Jesus Christ." It cannot be proven to anyone but yourself—and to God. But others around you probably recognize a very noticeable change in your character and behavior. Some of those who know you are a believer are, probably, also believers. A believer can usually detect whether or not another believer is for real just by the unity they have with one another in Christ, by their brotherly love for each other, by their testimonies, by their desire for sound doctrine, by their readiness to serve God, and their willingness to accept correction.

> My son, do not despise the chastening of the LORD, nor detest His correction; for whom the LORD loves He corrects, just as a father the son in whom he delights. (Proverbs 3:11–12)

> All Scripture is given by inspiration of God, and is profitable for doctrine, for reproof, for correction, for instruction in righteousness, that the man of God may be complete, thoroughly equipped for every good work. (2 Timothy 3:16–17)

> The way of a fool is right in his own eyes, but he who heeds counsel is wise. (Proverbs 12:15)

> A scoffer does not love one who corrects him, nor will he go to the wise. (Proverbs 15:12)

> The ear that hears the rebukes of life will abide among the wise. (Proverbs 15:31)

> He who answers a matter before he hears it, it is folly and shame to him. (Proverbs 18:13)

> The heart of the prudent acquires knowledge, and the ear of the wise seeks knowledge. (Proverbs 18:15)

> Listen to counsel and receive instruction, that you may be wise in your latter days. (Proverbs 19:20)

God tells us in His Word that He wants us to know Him (Hosea 6:6). To understand how to know Him a little more, a similarity can be made to understanding a fire: The essence of a fire requires three essential elements: 1) ignition, 2) fuel, and 3) air. Without any one of these three, there cannot be fire. All three are essential.

> Where there is no wood, the fire goes out. (Proverbs 26:20a)

The essence of God calls for three essential Persons: 1) The Father, Who, like the ignition, is the Instigator. He is the spiritual leader who gives instruction to the Son for what to do. When He said, "Let there be light," the Lord created the heavens. 2) The Son, Who like the fuel for the fire, is the Implementer. He always obeys the Father, not only to make the light, but also to create all creation, and so importantly for us; to suffer and die for all people—even to the point of death on the cross. 3) The Holy Spirit, Who, like the air needed for fire, is the Energizer. Fifty days after Christ's resurrection from the dead, the Spirit was sent by the Father through the Son to begin the church at Pentecost with a rushing mighty wind and subsequently to build up the church by filling all believers with Himself—the Holy Spirit (Acts 2:2). He also, by the Father's command, came upon the virgin Mary for the Father to beget His only Son, Jesus Christ.

> For that which is conceived in her [the virgin Mary] is of the Holy Spirit. (Matthew 1:20b)

God the Father sent God the Son from heaven to become flesh and dwell among us on the earth:

> "And the Word became flesh and dwelt among us" (John 1:14a).

And the Father had the Lord ascend back up to heaven forty days after His resurrection (Luke 24:51; Acts 1:3, 9).

> For I have come down from heaven, not to do My own will, but the will of Him who sent Me. (John 6:38)

I came forth from the Father and have come into the world. Again, I leave the world and go to the Father. (John 16:28)

Whoever denies the Son does not have the Father either; he who acknowledges the Son has the Father also. (1 John 2:23)

One of the reasons the Father sent His Son was to show us, by miracles, wonders, and signs that Jesus Christ is indeed the Son of God—the Messiah—the Savior—the Lord Jesus Christ (Acts 2:22). Further proof was when the Father had the Holy Spirit raise Jesus from the dead to live for evermore. (Romans 8:11)

He is not here; for He is risen. (Matthew 28:6)

He is risen! He is not here. (Mark 16:6b)

He is not here, but is risen! (Luke 24:6a)

Jesus said to him, "Thomas, because you have seen me, you have believed. Blessed are those who have not seen and yet have believed." (John 20:29)

But if the Spirit of Him who raised Jesus from the dead dwells in you, He who raised Christ from the dead will also give life to your mortal bodies through His Spirit who dwells in you. (Romans 8:11)

The Holy Spirit of God indwells every true believer to help them to stop practicing sin. The Spirit also indwells the all-encompassing Church of believers. Jesus Christ is the Head of the Church. The believers are the body of the Church. In God's plan, the last person to repent and come to believe in God as Three Persons will complete the building of the Church—the body of Christ. At that time (a time known only to the Father: Matthew 24:36; Mark 13:32; Acts 1:7), the Father will send His Son from heaven to the earth's atmosphere to take up (Rapture) and gather together the entire church body (1 Thessalonians 4:13-18; Romans 11:25-26; 1 Corinthians 15:52; Revelation 4:1)—every member of His body—and take them up into heaven. This will be the beginning of the end-times. His body is also His bride. The Groom loves His bride and would never allow His bride to suffer the wrath of God in the seven-year Tribulation period following the Rapture.

> Much more then, having now been justified by His blood, we shall be saved from wrath through Him. (Romans 5:9)

> For God did not appoint us to wrath, but to obtain salvation through our Lord Jesus Christ. (1 Thessalonians 5:9)

> And to wait for His Son from heaven, whom He raised from the dead, even Jesus who delivers us from the wrath to come. (1 Thessalonians 1:10)

> But of that day and hour no one knows, not even the angels in heaven, nor the Son, but only the Father. (Mark 13:32)

Paul the apostle writes,

> But concerning the times and the seasons, brethren, you have no need that I should write to you. For you [believers] yourselves know perfectly that the day of the Lord so comes as a thief in the night. For when they [unbelievers] say 'Peace and safety!' then sudden destruction comes upon them, as labor pains upon a pregnant woman. And they shall not escape. But you, brethren, are not in darkness, so that this Day should overtake you as a thief. (1 Thessalonians 5:1–4).

The reason the first verse says there is "no need that (Paul) should write to" (the believers) is because the believers will since seven years earlier have already been in heaven. Instead of judging believers for their sins, the Lord Jesus will reward them in heaven at the Judgment Seat of Christ. The day being spoken of here in 1 Thessalonians 5, the second verse—"the day of the Lord"— is the Second Coming (or Second Advent). The First Advent was when the Father sent Him from heaven to be miraculously born of the virgin Mary. The timing of the Second Advent—for Jesus to actually come down to earth in the flesh—is based upon His seven years previous descent to stop in the air and gather His Church together in the clouds to be with Himself from then on forever. The Book of Revelation gives vivid details of how the Church body will with Him to praise Him and glorify Him and will witness how the ones who rejected Him will suffer on earth. When He returns like a thief in the night, His bride, the Church, will be with Him.

The word *Rapture* is not in the Scriptures. However, the words *"caught up together"* translate to the same meaning, and are in 1 Thessalonians 4:17. Therefore, the word *Rapture* has become widely used by biblical scholars to refer to this awesome, joyful, soon coming event.

Soon following the Church being taken up, the seven-year tribulation period will begin. The first three and a half years will be a time of deception when the Antichrist makes a covenant for peace for the whole world—with a one world government. However, the last three and a half years will be the Great Tribulation period for the ones who are still alive and who rejected the Savior during their life so far on earth. At the end of the seven years of deception, extreme hardship and distress, the War of Armageddon will take place. The Lord of lords and King of kings, Jesus Christ, will win that war and cast the Antichrist and false prophet into unquenchable suffering in the Lake of Fire.

Again, the Groom will not let His bride of believers suffer in the soon-coming seven-year Tribulation. The Groom loves, protects, provides for, and rescues His bride. But the outsiders—that is, unbelievers—are about to enter into the seven-year Tribulation. The Book of Revelation describes in great detail not only the entire horrific Tribulation, but also provides a glimpse of what heaven will be like.

Revelation describes how the Church will be in heaven praising and worshiping the Lord. During that time, most unbelievers will be deceived by the false trinity: Satan, the Antichrist, and the false prophet. But in that Tribulation, a remnant—a few—including 144,000 Jews—will still have access to a Bible and will be able to learn, overcome, and be saved. They will attend the wedding feast when the Groom, Jesus Christ, has been married to His bride, the raptured Church. All believers of the Church Age—that is, since Pentecost, nearly two thousand years ago—both those who have died believing in Christ Jesus and those who are alive believing, will experience the Rapture explained by Paul the apostle:

> But I do not want you to be ignorant, brethren [all believers, male and female], concerning those who have fallen asleep [died as believers], lest you sorrow as others [unbelievers] who have no hope [no guarantee to be taken up to heaven]. For if we believe that Jesus died and rose again, even so God will bring with Him those who sleep in Jesus [those who died during the Church Age as believers]. For this we say to you by the word of the Lord, that we who are alive and remain until the coming of the Lord will by no means precede those who are asleep. For the Lord Himself will descend from heaven with a shout, with the voice of an archangel, and with the trumpet of God. And the dead in Christ will rise first. Then we who are alive and remain shall be caught up together with them in the clouds to meet the Lord in the air. And thus we shall always be with the Lord. Therefore comfort one another with these words. (1 Thessalonians 4:13–18)

The Church Age began at Pentecost, fifty days after Christ's resurrection from the dead (Acts 2:1–2), and will end at the Rapture of the Church.

Considering wisdom and just plain common sense, it is unimaginable that God would raise the dead believers from their graves to have them experience deception and suffering in the Tribulation period. 1 Thessalonians 4:16b–17 says,

> And the dead in Christ will rise first. Then we who are alive and remain shall be caught up together with them in the clouds to meet the Lord in the air. (1 Thessalonians 4:16b-17)

This is convincing of pre-tribulation Rapture. The Rapture happens in the twinkling of an eye (1 Corinthians 15:52). For the unbelieving ones, it also happens quickly like a thief in the night seven years later at Christ's Second Coming to the earth (1 Thessalonians 5:2). Then the Scripture goes on to say:

> But you, brethren [believing brothers and sisters in Christ], are not in darkness, so that this Day should overtake you as a thief. (1 Thessalonians 5:4)

> For God did not appoint us to wrath, but to obtain salvation through our Lord Jesus Christ, that whether we wake or sleep, we should live together with Him. (1 Thessalonians 5:9–10)

Our hope of salvation is being saved from the Tribulation period and being saved for eternal life together with our Groom, the Lord Jesus Christ.

The Rapture and eternal life are the hope of every believer. And God has always kept and always will keep His promises:

> In hope of eternal life which God, who cannot lie, promised before time began. (Titus 1:2)

2 Thessalonians 2:1–8 also confirms that the Tribulation is not for the Church. Rather, the Tribulation is a time of deception followed by suffering, reserved for the unbelievers:

Now brethren [all those believing in Christ], concerning the coming of our Lord Jesus Christ [His coming to the air for His bride, the Church] and our gathering together to Him [caught up together with them in the clouds to meet the Lord in the air], we ask you, not to be soon shaken in mind or troubled, either by spirit or by word or by letter, as if from us, as though the day of Christ had come [Paul the apostle is saying some of them might have thought they'd missed the Rapture]. Let no one deceive you by any means; for that Day will not come unless the falling away comes first [the falling away of the false-teaching apostate church, but in addition to the falling away, the Rapture must also happen before the Antichrist is revealed; see verses 7–8 as continued here and explained that the Church with the Holy Spirit is restraining him from being revealed], and the man of sin [Antichrist] is revealed, the son of perdition, who opposes and exalts himself above all that is called God or that is worshiped, so that he sits as God in the temple of God, showing himself that he is God. Do you not remember that when I was still with you I told you these things? And now you know what is restraining [the Holy Spirit who indwells all believers and therefore indwells the Body of believers is restraining the Antichrist while the Church is still on earth prior to the Rapture], that he [Antichrist] may be revealed in his own time. For the mystery of lawlessness is already at work; only He [the Holy Spirit indwelling the Church] who now restrains will do so until He is taken out of the way. [The Church with the indwelling Holy Spirit will go up in the Rapture, and the Church will no longer be on earth to restrain the Antichrist from starting the seven-year Tribulation period.] And the lawless one will be revealed, whom the Lord will consume with the breath of His mouth and destroy with the brightness of His coming. (2 Thessalonians 2:1–8)

The miraculous agreement of the Scripture is once again pointed out by this Thessalonians Epistle, written in AD50–51, compared to the prophecy written by Daniel in about 530 BC:

> He [the Antichrist] shall regard neither the God of his fathers nor the desire of women, nor regard any god; for he shall exalt himself above them all. (Daniel 11:37)

Christ's Second Coming will be at the end of the seven-year Tribulation, when He puts His feet on the earth and wins the battle of Armageddon, defeating Satan, the Antichrist, and the false prophet. The Antichrist and false prophet will be cast into the Lake of Fire. (Rev. 19:20) Then He will release and defeat Satan a second time at the end of His millennial reign. (Rev. 20:10)

The Spirit's methods of teaching us about the Rapture leave us in awe, revering our Savior. Hearing God's truths is not just sounds entering the ears. Hearing God's Word means absorbing, digesting, believing, and applying His pure truth and prescribed ways. The importance of listening and hearing, then, is paramount in making the right decision for our eternal futures.

> The hearing ear and the seeing eye, the LORD has made them both. (Proverbs 20:12)

> Incline your ear and hear the words of the wise, and apply your heart to my knowledge; for it is a pleasant thing if you keep them within you. (Proverbs 22:17–18a)

Chapter 6
WISDOM FOUND BY LISTENING

A key factor when we consider wisdom is the trait of listening. The words *listen*, *listened*, and *listens* are seen in the Bible over 350 times. To listen does not mean to give ear only to the sound being emitted.

"Listen: 1) to give ear; to attend closely with a view to hear. 2) To obey; to yield to advice; to follow admonition."[28]

Following is just a small sample of how listening has to do with wisdom:

> Listen to counsel and receive instruction, that you may be wise in your latter days. (Proverbs 19:20)

> Cease listening to instruction, my son, and you will stray from the words of knowledge. (Proverbs 19:27)

> Listen to your father who begot you, and do not despise your mother when she is old. Buy the truth, and do not sell it, also wisdom and instruction and understanding. (Proverbs 23:22–23)

> A wise man listens to advice. (Proverbs 12:15b NIV)

God wants us, His creation, to know Him. And when we know Him, we know He wants us to trust Him, to have faith in Him that He truly

---

[28] The original *American Dictionary of the English Language*, Noah Webster, 1828, s.v. "listen"

is our God, Creator, and Savior. When we know Him, we believe His Commandments are what make us knowledgeable that we have offended Him—that is, sinned against Him—by breaking at least one of His Ten Commandments.

> For whoever shall keep the whole law, and yet stumble in one point; he is guilty of all. (James 2:10)

The penalty for breaking God's Law is death. The reward for keeping His Law—that is, by being in God's view as having perfection—the reward is life.

> For the wages of sin is death, but the gift of God is eternal life in Christ Jesus our Lord. (Romans 6:23)

The Lord Jesus Christ took that penalty of death for us, even death by being nailed through His hands and feet to hang for six hours until dead on a wooden cross. When we believe that His shed blood satisfies our Father's wrath against us, and that His shed blood cleanses us of our sins, and that by His death we are given life, and that He was raised from the dead, then, by this believing, we are seen by God as having the same perfection as our God and Savior, the Lord Jesus Christ.

It can also be stated like this: When we believe in God being three Persons: the Father, the Son Jesus Christ, and the Holy Spirit, then, by the shed blood of Jesus, God forgives us and sees us as no longer being sinners, but as having the righteousness of God Himself. Paul the apostle spoke these words to some Greek philosophers in Athens:

> Truly, these times of ignorance God overlooked, but now commands all men everywhere to repent, because He has appointed a day on which He will judge the world in righteousness by the Man [Jesus] whom He has ordained [commissioned Him to die for us and to be the Judge]. He has given assurance of this to all by raising Him from the dead. (Acts 17:30–31)

Don't miss that last part of the verse: "raising Him from the dead." By the power to raise Christ Jesus from the dead, He has proven beyond any shadow of a doubt that He is indeed God. And this is the basis of the hope that every born again Christian holds. God promises to do the same for all who trust, believe, and have faith in Him. This is the beginning of wisdom. Revere Him. That center part of the Bible bears repeating:

> It is better to trust in the LORD than to put confidence in man. (Psalm 118:8)

If we listen to God and use the wisdom He provides, we are guaranteed to have abundance in our lives. Quoting the Lord Jesus:

> The thief [Satan] does not come except to steal, and to kill, and to destroy. I have come that they may have life, and that they may have it more abundantly.
> (John 10:10)

> My sheep [believers] hear My voice, and I know them, and they follow Me. And I give them eternal life, and they shall never perish; neither shall anyone snatch them out of My hand. (John 10:27–28)

Forgiveness of Sins

The essence of the Triune God being compared to fire can also be related to the necessity of being remorseful, forgiving, and loving in order to have an everlasting relationship. Our relationship with God puts our love for Him first, because He first loved us:

> We love Him because He first loved us. (1 John 4:19)

> But God demonstrates His own love toward us, in that while we were still sinners, Christ died for us. (Romans 5:8)

Since God loves us so much, considering wisdom, we should tell Him we are sincerely sorry for offending Him. When we do so with a sincere heart, He forgives us and chooses to not remember our past sins:

> I, even I, am He who blots out your transgressions for My own sake; and I will not remember your sins. (Isaiah 43:25)

> I have blotted out, like a thick cloud, your transgressions, and like a cloud, your sins. Return to Me, for I have redeemed you. (Isaiah 44:22)

> Says the LORD, "Though your sins are like scarlet, they shall be as white as snow; though they are red like crimson, they shall be as wool." (Isaiah 1:18b)

> Says the LORD ... "For I will forgive their iniquity, and their sin I will remember no more." (Jeremiah 31:34b)

> "In those days and in that time," says the LORD, "The iniquity of Israel shall be sought, but there shall be none; and the sins of Judah, but they shall not be found; for I will pardon those whom I preserve." (Jeremiah 50:20)

> None of his sins which he has committed shall be remembered against him. (Ezekiel 33:16a)

> For this is My covenant with them, when I take away their sins. (Romans 11:27)

> For I will be merciful to their unrighteousness, and their sins and their lawless deeds I will remember no more. (Hebrews 8:12)

> Then He adds, "Their sins and their lawless deeds I will remember no more." (Hebrews 10:17)

The *Choice Gleanings Calendar* from Gospel Folio Press for May 10, 2019, printed Psalm 130:3–4 along with Wm. H. Gustafson's comments:

> If You LORD, should mark iniquities, O Lord, who
> could stand? But there is forgiveness with You, that You
> may be feared. (Psalm 130:3–4)

Wm. H. Gustafson said, "We should never separate these two verses. Yes, God does know all our sins. Yet amazingly, He laid them on His Son—on the cross—so that forgiveness would be available to all who come to Him in simple faith. Our part is as simple as A-B-C: to admit we are sinners, believe Christ died for us, and confess Him as our Saviour. After salvation, if sin does tempt us we have His promise: 'If we confess our sins, he is faithful and just to forgive us our sins and to cleanse us from all unrighteousness.' 1 John 1:9"

In the New Testament, Christ is the long-awaited Messiah of the Old Testament. Jesus Christ is the Savior whom we need to get ourselves out of the sins we make against God and the repetitive offenses we commit against people like a coworker, a neighbor, or a spouse.

Being Born Again

Jesus said,

> "Most assuredly, I say to you, unless one is born again,
> he cannot see the kingdom of God." (John 3:3b)

What a vast change of life when one is born again. By accepting Him and the truth about God, believers know from that moment that they are changed people.

Truth cannot contradict itself. There's a story of a university professor who made this statement to his class: "There is no such thing as absolute truth." One of the students raised his hand and asked, "Is that a true statement?" The professor was stumped. If he answered yes, then he contradicted his own statement that there is no truth. And if he answered no, his original statement would then be nullified. The point here is that there is indeed, unquestionable, absolute truth.

New Spirit, New Heart, New Mind

> [Jesus said] "that whoever believes in Him should not perish but have eternal life. For God so loved the world [not the planet, but the people He created] that He gave His only begotten Son, that whoever believes in Him should not perish but have everlasting life." (John 3:15–16a)

Every earthly father who has ever procreated with a mother to conceive and give birth to a child, then has his own begotten child. If the couple has a child in their legal custody whom they did not procreate, then that is their adopted child. The Father God, through the Spirit of God and the virgin Mary, miraculously produced only One begotten Son. But the Father accepts those who believe in God as His adopted children.

> But as many as received Him, to them He gave the right to become children of God, to those who believe in His name: who were born not of blood, nor of the will of the flesh, nor of the will of man, but of God. (John 1:12–13)

> For as many as are led by the Spirit of God, these are sons of God. For you did not receive the spirit of bondage [slavery to sin] again to fear, but you received the Spirit of adoption by whom we cry out, "Abba, Father." (Romans 8:14–15)

God hates sin. God does not accept sin—that is, any offense against what He has commanded. He separates all sin from Himself. But for those who accept His invitation, He transferred the sin to Jesus on the cross. If the offender sincerely asks God to forgive that sin and truly believes in the one true God, not Allah, not Buddha, not the president of Korea, not a cow, not a carved piece of wood, a rock, or a tree, or a totem pole, or any other false god, then the sinner is forgiven by the shed blood of Jesus and is no longer bound for the Lake of Fire. Thus the offender is no longer separated from God but is redeemed back to being one with God. Jesus' death on the cross is sometimes referred to as His atoning death. Breaking down the word *atonement*, it becomes *at-one*-ment: "*At one with God; no longer separated from God, but redeemed—reconciled, again with God*" (emphasis added).

After sincerely asking God for forgiveness—even in silent prayer—and staying focused, reading and studying Scripture, believers experience that changes slowly take place in their behavior. At the first moment of believing, they become indwelt by the Holy Spirit. That is the moment when their sanctification process begins. *Sanctification* means set apart from the world's evil practices, and brought in to God's righteous practices. As believers get to know God better and better, the sanctification process continues along with their growth in their walk with the Lord. It all began when God's Word convinced them that they needed the Savior—that they could not possibly save themselves but must be born again. The believer, with a new heart and renewed mind, eventually becomes fully convinced and persuaded of God's truth—every Word of the flawless Bible.

> I will give you a new heart and put a new spirit within you. (Ezekiel 36:26a)
>
> I will put My Spirit within you and cause you to walk in My statutes. (Ezekiel 36:27a)
>
> He restores my soul; He leads me in the paths of righteousness for His namesake. (Psalm 23:3)

The new heart, indwelling Spirit, and renewed mind are the essence of being spiritually born again. To tie Ezekiel's saying "I will give you a new heart" to what Jesus said,

> "Most assuredly, I say to you, unless one is born again, he cannot see the kingdom of God" (John 3:3b)

Believers know the Bible is true, because they know they are changed persons. The believing changed person enters into a life-changing relationship with Jesus Christ and can begin to discern what the Bible is saying. It is no longer foolishness to the believer; rather it is understood as the wisdom that God intends it to be.

> But the natural man [the unbelieving man] does not receive [understand] the things of the Spirit of God, for they are foolishness to him; nor can he know them, because they are spiritually discerned.
> (1 Corinthians 2:14)

That's why believers are called born-again Christians. They're not saying "I'm holier than thou," because even though they may have been saved for many years, each one of them is still a sinner by having the nature of man—Adam. Believers do not habitually sin anymore; they do not practice sin. "He isn't sinless, but does sin less." They are just children when it comes to their new citizenship in God's kingdom. God calls them His adopted children.

> Behold what manner of love the Father has bestowed on us, that we should be called children of God! Therefore the world does not know us, because it did not know Him. (1 John 3:1)

Mary, the mother of Jesus, was a Jewish woman. The Jews were trying, unsuccessfully, to obey all the commandments of the law. This means they were under the law to try to save themselves by being totally obedient to all the commandments. They, like we, all failed.

> God sent forth His Son, born of a woman under the law, to redeem [bring back to being with God] those who were under the law, that we might receive the adoption as sons. And because you are sons, God has sent forth the Spirit of His Son into your hearts, crying out, "Abba, Father!" (Galatians 4:4b-6)

> For we know that the whole creation groans and labors
> with birth pangs together until now. Not only that, but
> we also who have the firstfruits of the Spirit, even we
> ourselves groan within ourselves, eagerly waiting for the
> adoption, the redemption of our body.
> (Romans 8:22–23)

We are eagerly waiting for Christ to return to the air to take us up to
heaven and receive our new bodies to house our souls.

> For our citizenship is in heaven, from which we also
> eagerly wait for the Savior, the Lord Jesus Christ, who
> will transform our lowly body that it may be conformed
> to His glorious body, according to the working by
> which He is able even to subdue all things to Himself.
> (Philippians 3:20–21)

> [The Father,] having predestined us [believers] to
> adoption as sons by Jesus Christ to Himself, according
> to the good pleasure of His will. (Ephesians 1:5)

> For it was fitting for Him [Jesus], for whom are all
> things and by whom are all things, in bringing many
> sons to glory, to make the captain of their salvation
> perfect through sufferings. For both He who sanctifies
> and those who are being sanctified are all of one, for
> which reason He is not ashamed to call them brethren.
> (Hebrews 2:10–11)

Brethren means believing brothers and sisters. Believers are His adopted
brothers and sisters. He is the only Son who was not adopted. He was
and is the only begotten Son of God.

Some of the best changes believers experience are fruits of the Holy
Spirit, Who lives within them. Two of these nine fruits are long-suffering
patience and self-control. During life before being saved by the Savior,
these fruits of the Spirit were sorely lacking.

The seven other fruits of the Spirit are awesome to obtain as well. All nine are given at once:

> But the fruit of the Spirit is love, joy, peace, longsuffering, kindness, goodness, faithfulness, gentleness, self-control. (Galatians 5:22–23)

* * *

The people who are in search of God need to know there are actually millions of false gods and false teachers among us, many of whom neither teach nor believe that Jesus was raised from the dead. The Saddūcees, members of a Jewish political sect, were enemies of Jesus, and they did not believe in the resurrection:

> For the Saddūcees say that there is no resurrection. (Acts 23:8a)

So "the Saddūcees are sad, you see." They have no hope. Much like atheists, "the problem is that atheism does not take away the pain; it only takes away the hope."[29]

But in regard to the resurrection of Jesus Christ from the dead, God tells us in His Word that a matter is resolved by two or three witnesses.

> "By the mouth of two or three witnesses the matter shall be established." (Deuteronomy 19:15b)

Over five hundred eyewitnesses saw Jesus during the forty days He was here on earth after He was raised from the dead. Paul the Apostle writes,

> For I delivered to you first of all that which I also received: that Christ died for our sins according to the Scriptures, and that He was buried, and that He rose again the third day according to the Scriptures, and

---

[29] *God's Not Dead 2*, directed by Harold Cronk, (2016, Pure Flix Entertainment, Scottsdale, Arizona) DVD, line by Pat Boone, (June 2019)

that He was seen by Cĕphas [Peter], then by the twelve. After that He was seen by over five hundred brethren at once, of whom the greater part remain to the present [present time of Paul's writing], but some have fallen asleep [died]. After that He was seen by James [the half-brother of Jesus], then by all the apostles. Then last of all He was seen by me also. (1 Corinthians 15:3–8a)

He was seen, He was seen, He was seen, He was seen.

> The Holy Spirit had given commandments to the apostles whom He had chosen, to whom He also presented Himself alive after His suffering by many infallible proofs, being seen by them during forty days and speaking of the things pertaining to the kingdom of God. (Acts 1:2b–3)

The apostles also saw Him ascend alive back up to heaven from where the Father had sent Him:

> Now when He had spoken these things, while they watched, He was taken up, and a cloud received Him out of their sight. (Acts 1:9)

Not only did He ascend back up to heaven but the Father promises to send Him back again for us—for us to also be resurrected to eternal life. This is our hope. And God does not lie.

> In hope of eternal life which God, who cannot lie, promised before time began. (Titus 1:2)

Since our omnipotent God created everything we see, it is not insurmountable for Him to perform these supernatural, powerful acts.

Jesus said,

> "With men this is impossible, but with God all things are possible" (Matthew 19:26).

The Rapture and the Great Tribulation

God, who's never broken a promise, promises to raise us from the dead and to take us up to be with Him.

Again, when the event called the Rapture occurs, all believers will be taken away, rapidly transported in the blink of an eye, and all unbelievers will be left behind to experience deception and tremendous suffering—even death, for many—especially during the last half of the seven-year Great Tribulation period. The Lord Jesus said,

> "For then there will be great tribulation, such as has not been since the beginning of the world until this time, no, nor ever shall be" (Matthew 24:21).

At the beginning of that seven-year Tribulation period, that false trinity consisting of Satan (imitating Father God), a human Antichrist (imitating the Savior, Son of God), and a false prophet (imitating the Holy Spirit of God) will deceive many into thinking there will be peace on earth. Anyone who does not submit to the Antichrist by taking a "mark" on the right hand or the forehead will not be allowed to buy or sell. Without that mark, it's going to be difficult to even buy food to eat.

The most horrible thing about taking the mark is that there is no more opportunity, no more hope. Taking that mark destines the unbeliever for the eternal Lake of Fire.

> He [Satan's Antichrist] causes all, both small and great, rich and poor, free and slave, to receive a mark on their right hand or on their foreheads, and that no one may buy or sell except one who has the mark or the name of the beast [the Antichrist] or the number of his name. Here is wisdom. Let him who has understanding calculate the number of the beast, for it is the number of a man: His number is 666. (Revelation 13:16–18)

In the previous chapter we read:

> Let no one deceive you by any means.
> (2 Thessalonians 2:3a)

Moving to verses 9-12 of that passage:

> The coming of the lawless one [Antichrist] is according to the working of Satan, with all power, signs, and lying wonders, and with all unrighteous deception among those who perish, because they did not receive the love of the truth, that they might be saved. And for this reason God will send them strong delusion, that they should believe the lie, that they all may be condemned who did not believe the truth but had pleasure in unrighteousness. (2 Thessalonians 2:9–12)

The Revelation of Jesus Christ provides a vivid prophecy of what John the apostle was envisioning to come forth in the very near future.

> In those days [the last half of the seven-year tribulation] men will seek death and will not find it; they will desire to die, and death will flee from them. (Revelation 9:6)

> If anyone worships the beast [the Antichrist] and his image, and receives his mark on his forehead or on his hand, he himself shall also drink of the wine of the wrath of God, which is poured out full strength into the cup of His indignation. He shall be tormented with fire and brimstone in the presence of the holy angels and in the presence of the Lamb. And the smoke of their torment ascends forever and ever; and they have no rest day or night, who worship the beast and his image, and whoever receives the mark of his name. (Revelation 14:9b-11)

> So the first went and poured out his bowl upon the earth, and a foul and loathsome sore came upon the men who had the mark of the beast and those who worshiped his image. (Revelation 16:2)

> Then the beast [the Antichrist] was captured, and with him the false prophet who worked signs in his presence, by which he deceived those who received the mark of the beast and those who worshiped his image. These two were cast alive into the lake of fire burning with brimstone. (Revelation 19:20)

With all the false teaching surrounding all of us, it is eternally, vitally important for each of us and for each of our loved ones to know the conclusive truth.

It needs to be understood that prophecies of things to come in the future were written in past tense because the prophets were writing about what had been given to them by God in visions of the future things to come. They wrote of what they saw in their visions.

There are numerous examples of what will happen that are given in prophecies of the Revelation of Jesus Christ:

> There was a great earthquake, such a mighty and great earthquake as had not occurred since men were on the earth. (Revelation 16:18b)

> And great hail from heaven fell upon men, each hailstone about the weight of a talent [about a hundred pounds]. (Revelation 16:21a)

This last Book of the Bible reveals that there will be numerous catastrophic events with many plagues. Rivers and spring water will be turned to blood; mountains will be leveled (Revelation 16:20).

In the very first of God's Ten Commandments, God our Creator says this:

"You shall have no other gods before Me" (Exodus 20:3).

God does not force Himself onto anyone. He simply states the one absolute truth for us to either accept or reject. Rejecting our Triune God with the Savior, the Lord Jesus Christ, is the only unforgivable sin in today's age.

* * *

If you drive across northwestern France, you will undoubtedly see military cemetery after cemetery—lined with what seems like perpetual crosses for grave markers of fallen soldiers from many nations. If each of those American warriors would have had any way of knowing how tremendously disheartened they would become with the changes going on in their home country, for which they had given the ultimate sacrifice of their own lives—how they, in fact, did give their all—they would be deeply saddened. And many brave warriors still living were left wondering why they'd seen their fellow soldiers die and why they, themselves, with artificial limbs were watching it all happen. We can only hope these courageous brothers and sisters in arms were saved and became brothers and sisters in Christ Jesus before they took their last breath.

The soldiers who were blessed to return alive from battle in Vietnam, thinking they would be welcomed home, were treated disrespectfully, with contempt. The media divided the nation by dwelling on the few bad apples in the barrel, which resulted in stereotyping the armed forces.

Speaking to one another about politics can be a touchy subject. But like everything else, whatever we do, we should see to it that God is glorified:

> Therefore, whether you eat or drink, or whatever you
> do, do all to the glory of God. (1 Corinthians 10:31).

WISDOM IN VOTING

If you think this is a touchy subject, just wait till chapters 10 and 11.

Many solid believing Christians think it's not important to vote since Romans 13:1 tells us that God appoints the governing authorities. The thought here is that no matter who they vote for, God is still going to control the minds of voters to elect whomever He has already appointed. However, many other solid believers do think it necessary to vote since some candidates may not render godly values and policies that agree with their faith. Neither way of thinking—to vote or not to vote—is incorrect.

> Let each be fully convinced in his own mind.
> (Romans 14:5b)

Wisdom has a lot to do with moral values. And politics also has a lot to do with moral values. Wisdom can simultaneously have a lot to do with both politics and moral values. Since these two entities can crash head-on, and knowing that our lives or those of our loved ones could end on this earth at any moment, it becomes imperative to pursue God's wisdom. Since we do not know when the end will happen, it is wise to think both short-term and long-term. Considering wisdom and using discernment derived from it, we can blend the two areas of judging political and moral values into our hearts and minds to do the right thing, come what may.

For a Christian writer, one might assume I'm about to become judgmental, which Christians should not do. But this believing Christian is also a citizen, a patriot, and a voter. Before voting, people should seriously consider wisdom. Why?

> Righteousness exalts a nation. (Proverbs 14:34a)

> Therefore, whether you eat or drink, or whatever you do, do all to the glory of God. (1 Corinthians 10:31)

Whatever you do includes how believers should consider God's will when voting.

> That you may walk worthy of the Lord, fully pleasing Him, being fruitful in every good work and increasing in the knowledge of God. (Colossians 1:10)

> For our citizenship is in heaven, from which we also eagerly wait for the Savior, the Lord Jesus Christ. (Philippians 3:20)

Although the eternal citizenship of believers is in heaven, during this temporary life on earth, they are not of the world but still in the world. No one knows when the Father will send His Son to take the believers up to heaven—that is, rapture them. Only the Father knows when that moment will happen:

> But of that day and hour no one knows, not even the angels of heaven, but My Father only. (Matthew 24:36)

The Rapture could happen before this is finished being written or, in the event the Lord tarries, before it's been read. But just in case Christ is not sent to Rapture us for a few more days, months, or years, we should consider our own eternal future and those of our loved ones. For the benefit of our children and grandchildren, we must provide them with sound doctrine so they will not be otherwise indoctrinated. Paul the apostle said in so many words that he loved his own countrymen so much that he would even forfeit his own salvation if they could be saved in his place:

> For I could wish that I myself were accursed from Christ
> for my brethren, my country-men according to the flesh.
> (Romans 9:3)

In that powerful statement of self-denial for eternal life in heaven, we can sense the utmost, highest form of human love. Most parents love their children so much that they want to spend eternity with them.

> Train up a child in the way he should go, and when he is
> old he will not depart from it. (Proverbs 22:6)

> For the LORD is good; His mercy is everlasting, and His
> truth endures to all generations. (Psalm 100:5)

> Children's children are the crown of old men, and the
> glory of children is their father. (Proverbs 17:6)

Even if a political policy is against God's prescriptions for a spiritually healthy nation or community, this agenda does not change the citizen's highest priority, which is to express our love of God by obeying, satisfying, and pleasing Him. Every believer's first love is for our God. When political policies steer away from God's prescribed way to behave, then the true believer gives honor and obedience to God and not to the country's rulers. But nothing keeps the Christian from praying for these types of leaders.

> For this reason we also, since the day we heard it, do
> not cease to pray for you, and to ask that you may be
> filled with the knowledge of His will in all wisdom and
> spiritual understanding. (Colossians 1:9)

> Finally then, brethren, we urge and exhort in the Lord
> Jesus that you should abound more and more, just as
> you received from us how you ought to walk and to
> please God. (1 Thessalonians 4:1)

> Beloved, do not believe every spirit, but test the spirits, whether they are of God. (1 John 4:1a)

In today's political domain, we are hearing some officials professing to be Christians. Their actions speak much louder than their words, however. Some are practicing sinful lifestyles, which cannot possibly allow them to be reconciled to God (unless they repent). Congressional representatives are making anti-Semitic remarks such as labeling people of Israel "Benjamins" and calling for the removal of aid from the nation of Israel. Many complained after we moved the US Embassy to Jerusalem. Meticulous study of Scripture will reveal that the God of Israel in the Old Testament is the same God of Christianity in the New Testament. Hebrews chapter 11 tells of Abel, Enoch, Noah, Abraham, and Sarah, who all became heirs of the righteousness that only comes by faith and believing in God. Believers will meet these famous people in heaven. But the Rapture and the seven-year Tribulation will come first.

> Little children [the believing, adopted children of God], it is the last hour; and as you have heard that the Antichrist is coming, even now many antichrists have come, by which we know that it is the last hour. (1 John 2:18)

The time of judgment is coming like a thief in the night, and the time is near. To God, a thousand years is like one day, according to Psalm 90:4 and 2 Peter 3:8.

> And every spirit that does not confess that Jesus Christ has come in the flesh is not of God. And this is the spirit of the Antichrist, which you have heard was coming, and is now already in the world. (1 John 4:3)

> Now I urge you, brethren, note those who cause divisions and offenses, contrary to the doctrine which you learned, and avoid them. For those who are such do not serve our Lord Jesus Christ, but their own belly, and by smooth words and flattering speech deceive the hearts of the simple. (Romans 16:17–18)

As we study the Word of God, we begin to see that the philosophy of a Christian *never judging* is a myth, a lie (emphasis added). It would be impossible for an assembly (a local church) to fulfill its Christ-given authority if it couldn't judge. It would be impossible even to live a safe and healthy life without judging. For who doesn't make judgment decisions concerning medicine, good or bad food, the right partner for life, the best value for your money, etc.? What government exists that doesn't have law and order and that judges its offenders? Who would want to live in a city without policemen? So, let's not be surprised that God authorizes his children to judge good and evil.[30]

Randy Amos writes about the four areas we are not to judge:

1. Heart motives: 1 Corinthians 4:3, 5
2. Outward appearance: John 7:24; 1 Samuel 16:7
3. Another's liberty: Romans 14:2, 13
4. Another's actions when you are doing the same thing: Matthew 7:1, 3

And he writes of the four areas we are to judge:

1. Ourselves: 1 Corinthians 11:31
2. Actions that are good or bad: Philippians 1:9–10
3. Doctrine: 1 Corinthians 14:29; 1 Thessalonians 5:20–21
4. Sin in the church: 1 Corinthians 5:12–13

Each of us has biases that influence our opinions and decisions. Whatever has indoctrinated us is what produces the bias within us. We can be indoctrinated by false teachings, or we can be indoctrinated by sound, moral, truthful principles—sound doctrine.

---

[30] *The Church: A Discipleship Manual for the Body of Christ*, pg 45: "To Judge or Not to Judge?" By R. P. Amos

With the rapid decline of morals, according to God's prescription, we can readily see in today's world why the Holy Spirit inspired Paul the apostle to write what follows in Romans chapter 1. Notice the downward spiral from not acknowledging God simply by seeing what He has created, to committing acts that become more and more immoral and evil:

> For the wrath of God is revealed from heaven against all ungodliness and unrighteousness of men, who suppress the truth in unrighteousness, because what may be known of God is manifest [revealed] in them, for God has shown it to them. For since the creation of the world His invisible attributes are clearly seen, being understood by the things that are made, even His eternal power and Godhead, so that they are without excuse, because, although they knew God, they did not glorify Him as God, nor were thankful, but became futile in their thoughts, and their foolish hearts were darkened. Professing to be wise, they became fools, and changed the glory of the incorruptible [eternal] God into an image made like corruptible [perishable] man—and birds and four-footed animals and creeping things. Therefore God also gave them up to uncleanness, in the lusts of their hearts, to dishonor their bodies among themselves, who exchanged the truth of God for the lie, and worshiped and served the creature rather than the Creator who is blessed forever, Amen. For this reason God gave them up to vile passions. For even their women exchanged the natural use for what is against nature. Likewise also the men, leaving the natural use of the woman, burned in their lust for one another, men with men committing what is shameful, and receiving in themselves the penalty of their error which was due. And even as they did not like to retain God in their knowledge, God gave them over to a debased mind, to do those things which are not fitting; being filled with all unrighteousness, sexual immorality, wickedness, covetousness, maliciousness;

full of envy, murder, strife, deceit, evil-mindedness; they are whisperers, backbiters, haters of God, violent, proud, boasters, inventors of evil things, disobedient to parents, undiscerning, untrustworthy, unloving, unforgiving, unmerciful; who, knowing the righteous judgment of God, that those who practice such things are deserving of death, not only do the same but also approve of those who practice them. (Romans 1:18–32)

The Gospel Folio Press's *Choice Gleanings Calendar* on May 17, 2019, quotes Job 4:8, which addresses this downward spiraling sin cycle described in that Romans 1 passage:

"They that... sow wickedness, reap the same" (Job 4:8b, d KJV).

Brian Cretney provided this commentary for that Job Scripture:

Sin begins as a *seed*. If it is not dealt with immediately, it becomes a *weed*, a weed that begins to choke out spiritual desires and nourishment. Before long that weed becomes a *deed*, manifesting itself in behaviour that is not honouring to the Lord. In time, that deed becomes a *need*, an addiction. It becomes hard to get through a day without fulfilling that sinful desire. That need begets *greed*, a pursuit of sin at all costs, leaving a trail of broken hearts and homes in the process. Hence the well-known truism: first, sin fascinates, then it assassinates. There is a two-fold antidote to this declining spiral: *feed* your soul the Word of God and *heed* the convicting prompts of the Holy Spirit to "flee also youthful lusts. (2 Timothy 2:22). (emphasis added)

When seeing how evangelical citizens vote,

"who, knowing the righteous judgment of God, that those who practice such things are deserving of death, not only do the same but also approve of those who practice them" (Romans 1:32).

This verse is probably partly responsible for persuading the voters to make their choices. Many politicians approve of those who practice such things; this is only one of several passages in which the Word of God condemns acts that are against His will. To Him, even approval of others performing these acts is an abomination. In fact, it outrages God. He hates sin and separates all sin from Himself.

> The High Priest [Jesus]... who is holy, harmless [innocent], undefiled, separate from sinners.
> (Hebrews 7:26b)

When "God gave them over to a debased mind," He caused them to lose reasoning ability. With no base, the mind has no foundation to be able to think and discern. Lack of reasoning ability and poor judgment ensue. There is no indwelling Spirit of God to help guard against temptations. Without the Spirit of God, Satan, who is wrestling against the Lord, can easily fire his weapons to weaken us and employ schemes to deceive us.

The good news is that God is just, forgiving, and loving; He patiently waits for sinners to repent and come to know Him who created them.

> Finally, my brethren, be strong in the Lord and in the power of His might. Put on the whole armor of God, that you may be able to stand against the wiles of the devil. For we do not wrestle against flesh and blood, but against principalities, against powers, against the rulers of the darkness of this age, against spiritual hosts of wickedness in the heavenly places. Therefore take up the whole armor of God, that you may be able to withstand in the evil day, and having done all, to stand. Stand therefore, having girded your waist with truth, having put on the breastplate of righteousness, and having shod your feet with the preparation of the gospel of peace; above all, taking the shield of faith with which you will

be able to quench all the fiery darts of the wicked one.
And take the helmet of salvation, and the sword of the
Spirit, which is the word of God; praying always with
all prayer and supplication in the Spirit.
(Ephesians 6:10–18a)

The wise advice God's Word is giving is to spend time daily with the
Lord in the Bible and in prayer. Accept His invitation to get to know
Him and trust in His wisdom-packed prescriptions.

Other Scriptures influence conservative and Christian voters as well:

I call heaven and earth as witnesses today against you,
that I have set before you life and death, blessing and
cursing; therefore choose life, that both you and your
descendants may live. (Deuteronomy 30:19)

Nearly two thousand years before Christ, God spoke to Abram (the Lord
changed his name to Abraham in Genesis 17:5 and changed the name
of Abraham's grandson Jacob to Israel in Genesis 35:10) concerning the
forthcoming nation of Israel:

Now the LORD had said to Abram:… I will make you a
great nation; I will bless you and make your name great;
and you shall be a blessing. I will bless those who bless
you, and I will curse him who curses you; and in you all
the families of the earth shall be blessed.
(Genesis 12:1a, 2–3)

Cursed be everyone who curses you [Israel], and blessed
be those who bless you! (Genesis 27:29b)

God put words into the mouth of Bālaam to bless Israel rather than to
curse Israel:

Blessed is he who blesses you, and cursed is he who
curses you. (Numbers 24:9b)

The psalmist Asaph prophesied that the enemies of God would attempt to wipe the nation of Israel off the map—and we still hear the chants of death to Israel and America today:

> Do not keep silent, O God! Do not hold Your peace, and do not be still, O God! For behold, Your enemies make a tumult; and those who hate You have lifted up their head. They have taken crafty counsel against Your people, and consulted together against Your sheltered ones. (Psalm 83:1–3)

The next verse, Psalm 83:4, is most disturbing, as we have now seen those elected to the US House of Representatives who, by their negative tone and rhetoric about Israel, could be somewhat connected with this verse:

> They have said, "Come, and let us cut them off from being a nation; that the name of Israel may be remembered no more." (Psalm 83:4)

When politicians denounce Israel, our strongest ally in the Middle East, it causes one to question their motive; when they denounce support for Israel, the above verses probably give weight to the God-honoring, Israel-supporting, evangelical, voting citizens.

Although suffering the presence of a few who resist and antagonize, a president's administration, when considering wisdom, should surround itself with several advisors who are believers.

> Where there is no counsel, the people fall; but in the multitude of counselors there is safety. (Proverbs 11:14)

> Righteousness exalts a nation, but sin is a reproach to any people. (Proverbs 14:34)

> How much better to get wisdom than gold! And to get understanding is to be chosen rather than silver. (Proverbs 16:16)

You shall not revile God, nor curse a ruler of your people. (Exodus 22:28)

Let every soul be subject to the governing authorities. For there is no authority except from God, and the authorities that exist are appointed by God. Therefore whoever resists the authority resists the ordinance of God, and those who resist will bring judgment on themselves. (Romans 13:1–2)

There's an ongoing movement to legalize the herb cannabis—marijuana. It began as if there weren't enough painkilling drugs available either on the shelf or given by a medical doctor's prescription. Then it progressed to legalization for recreational use. "Marijuana addiction is real."[31] "Marijuana over activates parts of the brain which can lead to a person losing their mental abilities."[32] People on the street call it getting "high."

What does our Creator have to say about either drinking too much wine or losing control?

And do not be drunk with wine, in which is dissipation [loss of self-control]; but be filled with the Spirit. (Ephesians 5:18)

Being filled with the Spirit provides self-control for a person. Indeed, self-control is one of the fruits of the Spirit.

Dissipation is defined as "debauchery, wildness, or indulgence."[33]

---

[31] DRUGABUSE.COM "Are You Really Addicted to Marijuana? Is Anyone?" (American Addiction Centers Editorial Staff), last part of 1st paragraph, (June 2019), https://drugabuse.com/marijuana-addiction/

[32] NIH National Institute on Drug Abuse, Marijuana DrugFacts, #Short-Term Effects and #Long-Term Effects, (June 2019) https://www.drugabuse.gov/publications/drugfacts/marijuana

[33] *The Strongest NIV Exhaustive Concordance*, (Zondervan, 1999), Greek to English Dictionary, pg 866, #861, s.v. "dissipation"

When people become intoxicated and are no longer sober, then loss of control of their senses can lead them to moral carelessness. Speech, vision, and the ability to walk can become impaired. This loss of self-control is in direct conflict with what the Ephesians 5:18 verse commands: "Do not be drunk with wine, in which is dissipation; but be filled with the Spirit." "Being filled with the Spirit means to 'be continually filled'."[34] A believer is not to be filled or intoxicated with loss of self-control, but is to be filled with the Holy Spirit.

God's Word provides His intent:

> "But the fruit of the Spirit is love, joy, peace, longsuffering, kindness, goodness, faithfulness, gentleness, self-control." (Galatians 5:22–23)

Notice the last of the fruits, the one that fills up, is self-control—the opposite of loss of control. "The *invisible power* of the Holy Spirit in those who are brought into living union with Christ (John 15:2–8) produces "the fruit of the Spirit." But the *visible* expressions of hidden lusts are the works of the flesh (emphasis added)."[35]

The Bible is consistent in pointing out the dangers of being intoxicated:

> Hear my son, and be wise; and guide your heart in the way. Do not mix with winebibbers, or with gluttonous eaters of meat; for the *drunkard* and the glutton will come to poverty, and drowsiness will clothe a man with rags (emphasis added). (Proverbs 23:19–21)

> Who has woe? Who has sorrow? Who has contentions? Who has complaints? Who has wounds without cause? Who has redness of eyes? Those who linger long at the wine, those who go in search of mixed wine. Do not look on the wine when it is red, when it sparkles in the

---

[34] *The King James Study Bible*, (Thomas Nelson, 1988), Liberty University comment pg 1838

[35] *Vine's Expository Dictionary*, (Thomas Nelson, 1997), pg 463, s.v. "fruit of the Spirit"

cup, when it swirls around smoothly; at the last it bites like a serpent, and stings like a viper. Your eyes will see strange things, and your heart will utter perverse things. Yes, you will be like one who lies down in the midst of the sea, or like one who lies at the top of the mast, saying: "They have struck me, but I was not hurt; they have beaten me, but I did not feel it. When shall I awake, that I may seek another drink?" (Proverbs 23:29–35)

Another Scripture details the detrimental effect that drunkenness has on a person's eternal destination.

Do you not know that the unrighteous will not inherit the kingdom of God? Do not be deceived. Neither fornicators, nor idolaters, nor adulterers, nor homosexuals, nor sodomites, nor thieves, nor covetous, nor drunkards, nor revilers, nor extortioners will inherit the kingdom of God. (1 Corinthians 6:9–10)

Envy, murders, drunkenness, revelries, and the like; of which I tell you beforehand, just as I also told you in time past, that those who practice such things will not inherit the kingdom of God. (Galatians 5:21)

In considering wisdom for our vote, we should consider whether the politician exhibits wisdom. At the same time, we should remember that if a politician digs up dirt on an opponent, those past actions could have been forgiven and corrected. God forgives if He is sincerely requested to do so by someone who is truly remorseful and repents. We should not dwell on the past; rather, we should consider who the person is now.

And you He made alive, who were dead in trespasses and sins, in which you once walked according to the course of this world, according to the prince of the power of the air [Satan], the spirit who now works in the sons of disobedience, among whom also we all once conducted ourselves in the lusts of our flesh, fulfilling the desires of the flesh and of the mind, and were by nature children of wrath, just as the others. (Ephesians 2:1–3)

For we ourselves were also once foolish, disobedient, deceived, serving various lusts and pleasures, living in malice and envy, hateful and hating one another. (Titus 3:3)

God has a plan. The Father is the only One who knows (Matthew 24:36; Mark 13:32) when He will send His Son to take up the Church of believers (the Rapture) and then turn Satan and his Antichrist loose to begin the seven-year Tribulation. Satan is the prince of the world, and he is a powerful force in offering up temptations to displease God. But God is in control of His creation. He allows godly and ungodly candidates to be elected, and the timing of Christ's return depends upon what stage of the Father's plan we are in. When the last believer, whom God is waiting upon, surrenders and accepts Jesus Christ as his personal Savior, it will be at that time that the next prophecy will be fulfilled—the next prophecy being the Rapture. God is waiting, and the believers are eagerly watching and waiting.

Right now, at this moment, we need to have a clear conscience and a clean heart in case the Rapture happens today. Only the Father knows when it will occur. If He tarries, we still need to be pleasing God. Looking to the future is important in our voting decisions. The time is right, right now.

The Boy Scout motto is "Be prepared." Being prepared is the key to success.

Wisdom and discernment that God provides for believers helps them to be prepared. When believers all bow before the Savior, who will judge us at His Judgment Seat, they will most likely want to have favor in His eyes. He knows how we will vote in the future, and He knows how we will have voted in the past. We must pay attention to the current events and know whether the proposed policies of the candidates are in line with God's will—that is, pleasing to God. To do so, we need to search for the truth in what the biased news outlets are telling us. All parties are biased, but obviously, one has a more pleasing course of action to suit God's desires.

In the event we die before the Rapture, the pleasing course of action is not for our own temporary pleasure, but the one that will be best for God and best for our children and grandchildren.

To discern, we use reasoning. We reason with respect to the value of our alternatives. To please God, we choose options that are most preferable to Him.

Admittedly, again, we all have bias, and we are all indoctrinated. But the eternal importance of being indoctrinated with sound doctrine cannot be overemphasized. Accepting the Lord Jesus as one's Savior is the most important decision anyone can ever make. Eternity is a long, long time. In fact, it is so long, it cannot be measured.

Our leaders need to make decisions that don't boost the enemy's morale. Giving financial aid at a time of tensions between them and us is just going to give them more confidence. Since "we are one nation under God," and we are "of the people, by the people, and for the people," we the people must, for a secure future, elect leaders who have a heart for God. Again, since we are a nation of the people, as constituents, we need our politicians to listen to God's wisdom, advice, and prescription. They must provide reasonable transparency in dealings with other nations.

Politicians need wise counselors to avoid making wrong decisions:

> Where there is no counsel, the people fall; but in the multitude of counselors there is safety. (Proverbs 11:14)

> Blessed is the nation whose God is the LORD.
> (Psalm 33:12a)

Looking back at history for voting with wisdom, we hear a lot about the push for socialism: This policy virtually mirrors major parts of Joseph Vladimir Stalin's 1936 Constitution for the Union of the Soviet Socialist

Republics (USSR). Two articles in chapter 10 of that constitution have been echoed by some US politicians: Article 120 provides the right to social insurance and free medical care; Article 121 ensures free schooling, even for higher education.[36]

Dictator Stalin killed nearly twenty million Soviet peasants[37] because they disagreed with his socialist policies—rather, his communistic dictatorial government control.

In some national parks, there are warnings for us not to feed the wild animals. The signs read: "Do not feed the wildlife. They will become dependent upon it." The same applies for free handouts to the animals called people. True, some citizens are unable to work due to disabilities, but there are social programs in place to help those who are genuinely in need. Socialism is seemingly for all, but not all are outwardly for socialism.

The USSR spent fifty years in the Cold War, attempting to globalize their system of communism, or socialism. The globe, if socialistic communism was colored red on a map, was progressing toward being all red. As a result, many people died, and thousands were Americans who fought to maintain our freedom of free enterprise, speech, press, religion, and the right to protect ourselves. One political candidate who promotes socialism has been called by the founder of Home Depot, "the enemy of all entrepreneurs."[38] We've been witnessing an attempt to have history repeat itself. We learn from history that we do not learn from history.

---

[36] Constitution (Fundamental Law) of the Union of Soviet Socialists Republics, (Red Star Press Ltd, London, 1978), "Marxists Internet Archive (2008)", article 120 and 121 (June 2019) https://www.marxists.org/reference/archive/stalin/works/1936/12/05.htm

[37] The New York Times "Major Soviet Paper Says 20 Million Died As Victims of Stalin", Bill Keller, February 4, 1989, (June 2019) https://www.nytimes.com/1989/02/04/world/major-soviet-paper-says-20-million-died-as-victims-of-stalin.html https://harvardmagazine.com/1999/07/right.stalin.html

[38] Fox Business, "Home Depot co-founder: Bernie Sanders is the 'enemy of every entrepreneur', 24 June 2019, (July 2019), https://www.foxbusiness.com/business-leaders/home-depot-cofounder-bernie-sanders-is-the-enemy-of-every-entrepreneur

Considering wisdom, it seems quite a gamble for humanity to attempt to repeat the socialist histories of North Korea, China, Venezuela, Hitler's Germany, and Stalin's Soviet Union. To maintain our God-given freedoms and rights, the vote requires judgment, discernment, and reasoning.

In relation to globalization, instead of nationalization, what wisdom does God's Word provide for us? The last Book of the Bible points out that in the end-times, during the Tribulation period, there will be a "one world government." John the apostle writes what he saw concerning one world headship in the vision of his prophecy:

> He [the false prophet] causes all, both small and great, rich and poor, free and slave, to receive a mark on their right hand or on their foreheads, and that no one may buy or sell except one who has the mark or the name of the beast [the Antichrist one world leader], or the number of his name. Here is wisdom. Let him who has understanding calculate the number of the beast [the Antichrist], for it is the number of a man: His number is 666. (Revelation 13:16–18)

Although the Antichrist will claim to be God, he is just a man, given power by Satan.

> For they are spirits of demons, performing signs, which go out to the kings of the earth and of the whole world, to gather them to the battle of that great day of God Almighty. (Revelation 16:14)

The "battle of that great day" is the soon-coming Battle of Armageddon. "The kings of the earth" are the one-world-government's military.

> And I saw the beast [the Antichrist man], the kings of the earth, and their armies, gathered together to make war against Him [Jesus Christ] who sat on the horse and against His army. (Revelation 19:19)

Christ's army is the raptured believers who, having been in heaven while the unbelievers were experiencing the seven-year Tribulation, return to the earth with the Lord Jesus.

> So they [the deceived unbelievers who missed the Rapture and were left behind] worshiped the dragon [Satan] who gave authority to the beast, saying, "Who is like the beast? Who is able to make war with him?" And he was given a mouth speaking great things and blasphemies, and he was given authority to continue for forty-two months [three and one-half years—half of the seven-year Tribulation period.] Then he opened his mouth in blasphemy against God, to blaspheme His name, His tabernacle, and those who dwell in heaven. It was granted to him to make war with the saints [the ones who, during the Tribulation, came to believe and were therefore not deceived] and to overcome them. And authority was given him [the Antichrist] over every tribe, tongue, and nation [one leader, one world government]. (Revelation 13:4–7)

The goal of Communism during the Cold War was to make the entire world socialist.

Paul the apostle writes in agreement with John the apostle:

> Let no one deceive you by any means; for that Day will not come unless the falling away comes first, and the man of sin is revealed, the son of perdition, who opposes and exalts himself above all that is called God or that is worshiped, so that he sits as God in the temple of God, showing himself that he is God. (2 Thessalonians 2:3–4)

The "man of sin" and "the son of perdition" is the Antichrist man.

> The coming of the lawless one is according to the working of Satan, with all power, signs, and lying

wonders, and with all unrighteous deception among those who perish, because they did not receive the love of the truth, that they might be saved.
(2 Thessalonians 2:9–10)

Yes, it is wise for politicians and voters to consider wisdom before making decisions or casting a ballot. Ask the question, "What does our God and Creator think of how I am voting?" God is in control. It is wise to listen to Him and not to rebel against Him. In terms of timing of prophesies being fulfilled, literally hundreds have been fulfilled to this point in time. The next prophesy to be fulfilled is the Rapture of believers to save them from suffering in the Tribulation and to continue their recently obtained eternal life. And next the revealing of the Antichrist man to rule over the ones who rejected Christ will be fulfilled. The prophesies that have been written and are to be fulfilled following the Rapture include the eternal suffering of those who choose to reject our God and Savior.

Quoting Harold Summers at a Morning Star Bible Camp men's conference: "Prophesies... [long pause as Harold scans the listeners looking each one in the eye]... will be... fulfilled."

To make a wise choice, one must keep abreast of current events. With today's technology, different news outlets can be found on the internet, and it doesn't take much time to look at both sides of the division between liberals and conservatives. Weigh and decide. Use discernment. Know the stances on policies, be aware of current events, and stay current in the Bible. Know what would grieve the Spirit of God and what would be pleasing to Him.

Government policies can tremendously impact our own and our children's lives. We the people can help steer the nation in the right direction by making sound decisions when we cast our vote. To do so, we should have knowledge of history, current events, and the agenda of the people running for office. The safety and eternal future of our children and grandchildren is at stake.

Chapter 8
UNFORESEEN FUTURE

Our armed forces troops of past wars could never imagine how disappointing the future of their beloved home country would become. They were fighting for freedom and hoping for eventual peace. However, the United States and other Western nations would soon be falling into attacks; injustices; violent riots; and political, religious, and further moral corruption. The cost of all the lives and limbs of the brave warriors who'd fought for preserving the freedom, rights and values of all US citizens would be an extremely high price to have paid for what would take place in the coming years.

On September 11, 2001, the biggest change ever in modern American lifestyle was broadcast on every news network. Those at home were glued to their televisions, watching in disbelief. Others waiting to board flights were made aware of the World Trade Center attack by airport television reports. Hearts sank. It seemed like a bad dream. All the lives that had already been sacrificed for our protection and freedom, and then this unjustified, violent, brutal, inhumane atrocity had to take place. It took the lives of three thousand innocent women, children, men, workers, airline crew, passengers, firefighters, police, and emergency medical technicians.

As the United States responded, it looked as if justice would be served. But then the mainstream media, with a seemingly political agenda, pushed against the administration's response. Even with the journalistic bias and political opposition, some headway was still made. But since 9/11, all have witnessed sudden increases in terrorism, violent protesting, drug deaths, sexual immorality, rape, and murder rates—even mass killings of innocent children in schools. It seems that many have been "turned over to debased minds"; things are going exactly as the Romans 1:18–32 passage describes the detailed, spiraling sin cycle.

Eight years later, many watched with great disappointment as the government repeated the way the Vietnam War ended. One would think we'd have learned from that history. Sometimes, we need to hit the pause button to look back at where we've been to better understand to where it is we are headed. Looking back:

In 1973, at the end of involvement in Vietnam, with huge media pressure sparking protests, all US troops were brought back home. It was left up to the South Vietnamese to hold off the North Vietnamese communist aggression. Congress promised the South we would return if they could not defend themselves.

US politicians did not keep that promise. South Vietnam fell in 1975. The United States did nothing to prevent it. It's still sad to picture Vietnamese mothers in tears, handing their infants over the fence to unknown futures at the US Embassy in Saigon so their children could join the refugees called "boat people." The reason the mothers were handing their babies over was to keep them from having to be raised in a future Communist totalitarian fascist dictatorship. Beyond the deep emotions, the moms must have heard of Margaret Thatcher's famous quote: "The problem with socialism is that you eventually run out of other people's money."[39]

Sixteen years later, America experienced a dramatic change in the way to do battle from more of those who impose sweeping changes in our way of governing, when the Islam extremists began a new war. But there were similar circumstances.

---

[39] USA Today, "Thatcher's quotes sting, startle and stick", USA Today research April 8, 2013, #On economics, 1st quote, (June 2019) https://www.usatoday.com/story/news/world/2013/04/08/thatcher-quotes/2062835/

Before a claim to victory near the final stages of the fight against radical Islamic terrorism (a term deemed politically incorrect by extremists), our troop strength was depleted; many soldiers came back home, and a few were left behind. At that time, this only resulted in putting the fewer soldiers in greater harm's way. Moreover, it allowed the enemy to build up and continue penetration of other countries around the world and further penetrate our homeland.

Even the labels ISIS and ISIL became confusing to most people, some of whom had the impression that one was more correct than the other. But the bare fact is that both have to do with radical Islamic terrorism. ISIS are radical extreme terrorists from the Islamic States of Iraq and al-Sham—or Iraq and Greater Syria. Together, they are called the Islamic State of Iraq and Syria: ISIS. But another name for Greater Syria is the Levant; thus the term ISIL: Islamic State of Iraq and the Levant. Considering wisdom, no matter how we say it, being politically correct does not make the radical Islamic extreme terrorists go away.

Not only had ways of war transformed, but also governing officials from within promoted socialism. Political correctness had become a disease.

We are all born equal, but we do not all remain equal. A big problem with socialism is that it can eventually lead to communism. The problem with communism is that it depends on each person having the same initiative as everyone else. Widening differences due to our experiences, some people develop the incentive to work hard, but others do not want to work at all. Others are at different stages in between. Even in our thriving capitalistic society, there are already government programs in place to financially assist citizens who are in legitimate need—that is, if they will accept the support. Some who are eligible turn it down, because they desire to earn their keep.

What does wisdom say about those who do not want to work?

> Go to the ant, you sluggard! Consider her ways and be wise, which, having no captain, overseer or ruler, provides her supplies in the summer, and gathers her

food in the harvest. How long will you slumber, O sluggard? When will you rise from your sleep? A little sleep, a little slumber, a little folding of the hands to sleep—so shall your poverty come on you like a prowler, and your need like an armed man. (Proverbs 6:6–11)

As vinegar to the teeth and smoke to the eyes, so is the lazy man to those who send him. (Proverbs 10:26)

The soul of a lazy man desires, and has nothing; but the soul of the diligent shall be made rich. (Proverbs 13:4)

The lazy man will not plow because of winter; he will beg during harvest and have nothing. (Proverbs 20:4)

The lazy man is wiser in his own eyes than seven men who can answer sensibly. (Proverbs 26:16)

For even when we [apostles] were with you, we commanded you this: If anyone will not work, neither shall he eat. (2 Thessalonians 3:10)

Our government did not learn from the Vietnam history. The politicians probably meant well, bringing troops home from Iraq and Afghanistan, saying that their own people—like South Vietnam's own people—could hold off the enemy. And they did not learn from Napoleon that "weapons are not what win wars—it is spirit that wins wars." Both Vietnam and the Middle East nations were calloused with war, and their spirit was drained. History must be paid attention to. To see ahead, we need to look back.

The government failed all the high-spirited US soldiers who'd sacrificed their very lives to put America in the lead in both wars—and then seemingly gave up and weakened our forces by diminishing the troop strength. They essentially fed the enemy a spirit to forge ahead. The terrorists' cells grew and spread like wildfire. Terrorists of Al Qaeda began replenishing, and ISIS grew and rapidly spread across the globe.

After ISIS caliphates were minimized, the president was criticized for removing troops from northern Syria, where the Kurds were located. But when we look closely at the reasoning for getting US forces out from between two of our allies, Turkey and the Kurds, we see that the rationale had to do with how long the two have been fighting. It is an endless war that no one can halt. The founder of the Arab nations is Ishmael, the son of Abram and Hagar. God's Word speaks of Ishmael thus:

> He shall be a wild man; His hand shall be against every man, and every man's hand against him. And he shall dwell in the presence of all his brethren. (Genesis 16:12)

> He shall beget twelve princes, and I will make him a great nation. (Genesis 17:20b)

Sure enough, the wars are still going on, and have been going since Ishmael started them twenty-one hundred years before Christ. That's four thousand years ago. The factions of Islam have been fighting each other since the Qur'an was written, six hundred years after Christ was crucified and resurrected. It's not that we want to see all those innocent people get slaughtered in those wars. Rather, since it cannot be stopped, we do not want our own loved ones to be added to the casualties. And that's probably why the president got the US troops out of harm's way. God said it would be so, and neither anything nor anyone can change the circumstances. This is totally different than the wars against communism and terrorism. This forever ongoing battle is part of God's plan to come to the end of the ages. "The time is near."

Wisdom Says Lawmakers Should Uphold the Law

Considering wisdom, if our country is suffering from terrorist attacks and lacks the political will to stop them, then the law-breaking politicians need to suffer the penalty. They need to be replaced. Justice needs to be served.

Our lawmakers need to protect our own nation's citizens from an invasion both of bad and of good people crossing the border illegally. If they do not uphold the law, the title of "lawmaker" is an oxymoron. Additionally, allowing law breakers into our nation without consequence affects the safety of our citizens.

Weigh and decide. If we support and finance radical terrorist organizations that persecute and mutilate innocent bystanders, ram crowds with vehicles, set off suicide explosions in public places, and literally cut off people's heads, we need to employ wisdom.

It seems wise and reasonable to stop human trafficking of young women and children, dangerous drug smugglers, murderous gangs, and just plain illegal intrusion into our country.

Considering our children's futures, it is wise to consider wisdom in every decision. Wisdom must be passed from generation to generation.

The word *eternity* is the longest word in our language. If you go north, you eventually come to an end at the North Pole. If you head south, your southbound journey stops at the South Pole. But if you go east or west, you never get to the end:

> For as the heavens are high above the earth, so great is His mercy toward those who fear Him; as far as the east is from the west [forever], so far has He removed our transgressions from us. (Psalm 103:11–12)

Eternity is what matters. Jesus said to His disciples:

> Do not worry about your life, what you will eat; nor about the body, what you will put on. Life is more than food, and the body is more than clothing. (Luke 12:22–23)

> Who of you by worrying can add a single hour to your life? If you cannot do this very little thing, why do you worry about the rest? (Luke 12:25–26 NIV)

Wisdom says to think, to discern, and to use reasoning and good judgment. Jesus says,

> "Do not judge according to appearance, but judge with righteous judgment" (John 7:24).

> You shall do no injustice in judgment.... You shall have honest scales.... Therefore you shall observe all My statutes and all My judgments, and perform them: I am the LORD. (Leviticus 19:35a, 36a, 37)

> You shall do no injustice in judgment. You shall not be partial to the poor, nor honor the person of the mighty. (Leviticus 19:15)

> These things also belong to the wise: It is not good to show partiality in judgment. (Proverbs 24:23)

> You shall appoint judges... and they shall judge the people with just judgment. (Deuteronomy 16:18a, c)

> To do righteousness and justice is more acceptable to the LORD than sacrifice. (Proverbs 21:3)

Classified information doesn't seem to matter to some, but for experienced military personnel, having been held responsible for its use and protection while serving their country, it demands an explanation and equal justice: Soldiers who compromise even one document of classified information with negligence or carelessness would be on trial by court-martial.

There are three categorizations of classified material: Confidential, Secret, and Top Secret. A candidate for the presidency was found to have been "careless" at all three levels of classification. The law states that negligent handling of any classified information constitutes a crime.

If one simply takes the time to look up the definition of *negligent*, it would be found to be synonymous with *careless*. The Department of

Justice has historically been noted for having wisdom, but it appears that something went awry.

The New Webster Encyclopedic Dictionary gives this definition: "careless, free from care or anxiety; heedless; negligent, unthinking, inattentive."[40]

The Top Secret classified level "shall be applied to information, the disclosure of which, reasonably could be expected to cause exceptionally grave damage to the national security" of the United States of America.[41]

It's been many times said, "The resistance hates the president more than they love the country." What does God's Word say about resisting the governing authority?

> Let every soul be subject to the governing authorities. For there is no authority except from God, and the authorities that exist are appointed by God. Therefore whoever resists the authority resists the ordinance of God, and those who resist will bring judgment on themselves. (Romans 13:1–2)

God is in control. It is wise to listen to Him and not to rebel against Him.

If the person you vote for does not win the election, it can be frustrating, but it's time to move on and try to be obedient to the elected officials who are in office. Of course, we can become very disappointed, and disagreements about policy often ensue. However, we need to love one another and not hold a grudge. One of the most quoted verses in the New Testament from the Old Testament comes from Leviticus:

> You shall not take vengeance, nor bear any grudge against the children of your people, but you shall love your neighbor as yourself: I am the LORD. (Leviticus 19:18)

---

[40] *The New Webster Encyclopedic Dictionary of the English Language*, (Consolidated Book Publishers Chicago - Processing & Books, Inc.), s.v. "careless"

[41] Security Classification of Information: Table of Contents, Chapter 7 CLASSIFICATION LEVELS, Introduction item (1), (May 2019), https://fas.org/sgp/library/quist2/chap_7.html

You may dislike the way the president talks or think he cannot be forgiven for past shortcomings, but this does not justify hatred for him.

> Whoever hates his brother is a murderer, and you know
> that no murderer has eternal life abiding in him.
> (1 John 3:15)

Looking with honesty at any president's past will definitely reveal some faults.

> As it is written: There is none righteous, no, not one.
> (Romans 3:10)

> For all have sinned and fall short of the glory of God.
> (Romans 3:23)

Take notice here that Romans 3:23 does not say, "All have sinned except for the pope or except for the president or except for the preacher," but *all* have sinned and fall short of the glory of God.

> Death spread to all men, because all sinned.
> (Romans 5:12b)

> If you have anything against anyone, forgive him,
> that your Father in heaven may also forgive you your
> trespasses. But if you do not forgive, neither will your
> Father in heaven forgive your trespasses.
> (Mark 11:25b-26)

One would never have thought the nation could sink to such a level of ungodliness. The justice system has almost come to reek to high heaven with the double standards applied to some politicians compared to others and even to military heroes and ordinary citizens. Our ancestors would come out of their graves to fight if they weren't already gone. But we need to pray for our politicians, forgive them, and love them with brotherly love.

Chapter 9
FORGIVE AND FORGET

This piece of absolute truth is important at this point: If you want to look into anyone else's past to find dirt, you'll find it.

> For all have sinned and fall short of the glory of God.
> (Romans 3:23)

If anyone reading this right now claims to have never used God's name in vain, or never told a lie, or never looked at another person with lust, or never taken anything that did not rightfully belong to them, then they could boast that they do not need the sinless Savior who gave His life on the cross to take our punishment. They, in effect, would be saying, "I can achieve total righteousness without Him. Jesus Christ died for nothing."

> I do not set aside the grace of God; for if righteousness comes through the law [being able to keep the Ten Commandments], then Christ died in vain.
> (Galatians 2:21)

If anyone looks for faults in this author's past, the dirt will definitely be found. This writer is not even near perfect. And we've never had a perfect president. On this earth, there isn't even such a thing as a perfect preacher. But if a person has the intestinal fortitude—the courage—to sincerely confess sins to God and to repent and be born again, then that person's sins are forgiven by God. The forgiveness comes through the shed blood of Jesus Christ.

To Him who loved us and washed us from our sins in
His own blood. (Revelation 1:5b)

If we say that we have no sin, we deceive ourselves, and the
truth is not in us. If we confess our sins, He [God] is faithful
and just to forgive us our sins, and to cleanse us from all
unrighteousness. If we say that we have not sinned, we
make Him a liar, and His word is not in us. (1 John 1:8–10)

If Jesus can pour out His blood to forgive us, we should be willing to swallow
our pride and sincerely admit, "I am guilty." Furthermore, we should say
to one another, "I forgive you." These four three-word sentences are such
very important words in our language: "I was wrong," "I am sorry," "I
forgive you," and "I love you." Each of these can be extremely difficult to
say. But once spoken from the bottom of the heart, what a tremendous relief.
Sincerity cannot be overemphasized. Only God knows our hearts.

Considering wisdom, when God forgives our past, He chooses not to
remember. This is another reason some people seem to be surprised
at a president's faithful supporters. An unbelieving person cannot
comprehend that a believer's past is forgiven.

For I will be merciful to their unrighteousness, and their
sins and their lawless deeds I will remember no more.
(Hebrews 8:12)

And why do you look at the speck in your brother's eye,
but do not consider the plank in your own eye? Or how
can you say to your brother, "Let me remove the speck
from your eye"; and look, a plank is in your own eye?
Hypocrite! First remove the plank from your own eye,
and then you will see clearly to remove the speck from
your brother's eye. (Matthew 7:3–5; Luke 6:41–42)

In some situations, considering wisdom and history, it is wise not to
look back, rather to look ahead. The times we look back should be for
looking where we've been to better understand where we are going. But

for life in general, considering wisdom and what is eternal, it is usually best to look ahead—to be prepared. Look ahead to eternity.

Prepare to meet your God. (Amos 4:12b)

Seek the LORD while He may be found, call upon Him while He is near. (Isaiah 55:6)

For it is time to seek the LORD (Hosea 10:12b)

"Therefore you also be ready, for the Son of Man [Jesus, who is also the Son of God] is coming at an hour you do not expect." (Luke 12:40)

Therefore God also has highly exalted Him and given Him the name which is above every name, that at the name of Jesus every knee should bow. (Philippians 2:9–10a)

For it is written: "As I live, says the LORD, every knee shall bow to Me, and every tongue shall confess to God." (Romans 14:11)

And there is no creature hidden from His sight, but all things are naked and open to the eyes of Him to whom we must give account. (Hebrews 4:13)

I have hope in God, which they themselves also accept, that there will be a resurrection of the dead, both of the just and the unjust. (Acts 24:15)

Yes, the unjust—the unsaved—will be raised back, but for judgment. Jesus told John to write about the future events that will take place in the end-times; in the Revelation of Jesus Christ, the following vision was given to John:

And I saw the dead, small and great, standing before God, and books were opened. And another book was opened, which is the Book of Life. And the dead were judged according to their works, by the things which were written in the books. The sea gave up the dead who were in it, and Death and Hādēs delivered up the dead who were in them. And they were judged, each one according to his works. Then Death and Hādēs were cast into the lake of fire. This is the second death. And anyone not found written in the Book of Life was cast into the lake of fire. (Revelation 20:12–15)

Most have heard the sayings "Look before you leap" and "No one gets out of this alive" (except possibly for those who are alive and remain at the Rapture). We all need to look before either death takes us down or the Rapture takes us up. We need to be ready because either death or the Rapture could happen at any moment.

"The time is near" (Revelation 1:3b).

Behold, now is the accepted time; behold, now is the day of salvation. (2 Corinthians 6:2b)

For you yourselves know perfectly that the day of the Lord so comes as a thief in the night. (1 Thessalonians 5:2)

Remember therefore how you have received and heard; hold fast and repent. Therefore if you will not watch, I will come upon you as a thief, and you will not know what hour I will come upon you. (Revelation 3:3)

For unbelievers, the judgment will be for conscious, eternal suffering. For believers, the judgment will be for rewards in heaven:

And as it is appointed for men to die once, but after this the judgment, so Christ was offered once to bear the sins of many. To those who eagerly wait for Him He will appear a second time apart from sin, for salvation. (Hebrews 9:27)

How Can Believers Prove They Are Saved?

Johnny Cash recorded a song in which he was asked how he knew he was saved. The first verse goes like this:

> There are some people... who say we cannot tell
> Whether we've been saved or... whether all is well
> They say we only can hope... and trust that it is so
> Well, I was there when it happened... so I guess I ought
> to know.

Alfred H. Ackley (1887-1960) wrote the hymn "He Lives" that ends with the words:

> You ask me how I know He lives? He lives within my
> heart.

That pretty much tells it like it is. We do know we're saved when we submit and allow God to save us. Only God knows the heart; it's near impossible to prove to an unbelieving person that you've been saved. However, believers know they are changed and experience a new relationship with Jesus Christ. The saved man himself knows he is behaving differently and responding to life's everyday changing circumstances in a more pleasing way to God.

We can be happy for our ancestors who were saved before they died and for the fact that we who believe as they did (and still do) will be in the place where there is no more pain, no more sorrow, and no more tears. We thank our God above for His plan to bring all who believe in Him back to Himself.

> And they sang a new song, saying: "You [Jesus] are
> worthy.... For You were slain, and have redeemed us to
> God by Your blood" (Revelation 5:9a, b)

> "And God will wipe away every tear from their eyes;
> there shall be no more death, nor sorrow, nor crying.

There shall be no more pain, for the former things have passed away." Then He who sat on the throne said, "Behold, I make all things new." And He [Jesus] said to me [John the Apostle], "Write, for these words are true and faithful." (Revelation 21:4–5)

Upon recognizing we are saved, believers come to realize their most important possession is eternal life.

The most import inheritance we can leave for our children is eternal life.

> With Your hand from men, O LORD, from men of the world who have their portion in this life, and whose belly You fill with Your hidden treasure. They are satisfied with children, and leave the rest of their possession for their babes. (Psalm 17:14)

> And whatever you do, do it heartily, as to the Lord and not to men, knowing that from the Lord you will receive the reward of the inheritance; for you serve the Lord Christ. (Colossians 3:23–24)

> But the mercy of the LORD is from everlasting to everlasting on those who fear Him, and His righteousness to children's children. (Psalm 103:17)

> And His mercy is on those who fear Him from generation to generation. (Luke 1:50)

> We will not hide them from their children, telling to the generation to come the praises of the LORD, and His strength and His wonderful works that He has done. For He established a testimony in Jacob, and appointed a law in Israel, which He commanded our fathers, that they should make them known to their children; that the generation to come might know them, the children who would be born, that they may arise and declare

them to their children, that they may set their hope in God, and not forget the works of God, but keep His commandments. (Psalm 78:4–7)

Only the Lord Jesus could "keep all His commandments." But simply by believing in God and not rejecting Him, God sees the believer as one who keeps those commandments through the forgiveness of our sins by the washing with His blood. Oh, how God wants us to know Him and believe in Him and love Him. We express our love by being obedient to Him. Jesus said:

If you love Me, keep My commandments. (John 14:15)

He who has My commandments and keeps them, it is he who loves Me. (John 14:21a)

But My righteousness will be forever, and My salvation from generation to generation. (Isaiah 51:8b)

Tell your children about it, let your children tell their children, and their children another generation. (Joel 1:3)

What is it we should tell our children? We should tell them the same thing we say when we are asked how we can prove we are saved. We should tell them that we believe the Gospel message is true:

For I delivered to you first of all that which I also received: that Christ died for our sins according to the Scriptures [Psalm 22:15; Isaiah 53:5–12], and that He was buried, and that He rose again the third day according to the Scriptures [Psalm 16:9–11]. (1 Corinthians 15:3–4)

Christians believe that Jesus died and was raised back to life on the third day, following His crucifixion. Based upon our belief, God promises to also raise us from the dead. Why should we believe it? There are many reasons, some of which bear repeating.

First, in today's court proceedings, the eyewitness accounts are what bring the truth to light. This is based upon what was written in this next verse over thirty-four hundred years ago in God's Word:

> By the mouth of two or three witnesses the matter shall be established. (Deuteronomy 19:15b)

Then, fifteen hundred years later, not just two or three witnesses, but over five hundred_eyewitnesses are recorded to having witnessed the Lord Jesus Christ resurrected back to life from the dead. We need to tell our children:

> After that He was seen by over five hundred brethren at once, of whom the greater part remain to the present [at the time Paul the apostle wrote this], but some have fallen asleep [died]. (1 Corinthians 15:6)

For the true believer, this settles it, or establishes the matter. Indeed, Jesus Christ was raised back to life from death, as was witnessed. It does not matter if the witnesses saw this happen nearly two thousand years ago, last year, last week, or yesterday. The witnesses saw Him alive, raised from the dead, and it is truthfully reported in the Bible.

Not only the eyewitness accounts provide facts to convince us, but also each believer has become a changed person. The changed person knows for sure the Bible is absolutely true. At the moment they read or heard, absorbed, and digested the commandments that they'd broken and then realized they were guilty, at that moment when they repented and prayed for forgiveness for their offenses, they no longer had the old desire to practice a sinful lifestyle.

Jeremiah prophesied about 2,650 years ago:

> And you will seek Me and find Me, when you search for Me with all your heart. I will be found by you, says the LORD. (Jeremiah 29:13–14a)

The prophet Ezekiel quoted God over twenty-six hundred years ago:

> I will give you a new heart and put a new spirit within you. (Ezekiel 36:26a)

> I will put My Spirit within you and cause you to walk in My statutes. (Ezekiel 36:27a)

Then 630 years later, the Lord Jesus said,

> "Seek, and you will find" (Matthew 7:7b; Luke 11:9).

> Most assuredly, I say to you, unless one is born again, he cannot see the kingdom of God. (John 3:3)

Believers know they are born-again Christians because they are changed, with a new heart with the indwelling Spirit. They still have the old nature of Adam's DNA in their system, but they also have the Spirit of God indwelling them to overcome the world's temptations, and even though they are sinners, they now practice obeying God's commandments. They may not be able to keep the law completely, but at least they recognize when they are going in the wrong direction or get immoral thoughts, and the Spirit within them quickly puts the Savior who died for them in their thoughts. Since Jesus separates sin from Himself, the sinful thoughts leave these believers, and the indwelling Holy Spirit turns them around and corrects their corrupt impulse.

Third, believers can now understand much of what they read in the Bible. Prior to being saved, they most likely thought the Bible was foolishness and impossible to comprehend. And that's exactly what God's Word says will be the case for an unbelieving person. Paraphrasing the beginning of 1 Corinthians 2:14, the unsaved man does not understand the Words of God—in the Bible—for they are foolishness to him; nor can he know them, because they are spiritually discerned. Now that the Spirit indwells the believers, God's Word has become clear to them.

They cannot possibly profess to know everything, but as they grow in faith, they learn more and hunger for more.

Fourth, the unity shared by fellow believers proves the truth by the fact that they can understand each other when they love one another and speak of God's truths in His understandable terms. Believers are greatly blessed to hear one another's testimonies.

> Behold, how good and how pleasant it is for brethren to
> dwell together in unity! (Psalm 133:1)

> We are of God. He who knows God hears us; he who is
> not of God does not hear us. By this we know the spirit
> of truth and the spirit of error. (1 John 4:6)

Fifth, the prophesies that have been fulfilled provide overwhelming proof of God's truth. For example, Isaiah prophesied two hundred years before King Cyrus decreed Israel's freedom—well before Cyrus was born—that a king named Cyrus would be the king to decree the release of the Israelites from Babylonian captivity. Then, two hundred years after Isaiah's 740 BC prophecy, sure enough, in 539 BC, King Cyrus ruled that the Israelites should be set free and returned back home (Isaiah 44:28, 45:1; 2 Chronicles 36:22–23). The finite details of the prophecies of the arrest, trial, beatings, mocking, crucifixion, and resurrection of Jesus Christ in Isaiah chapter 53 are also valid proof of fulfillment as seen in the New Testament Gospels of Matthew, Mark, Luke, and John.

Rejecting Jesus Christ does not make Him go away. Why do people reject Him? Could it be peer pressure? This is not talking about teenage peer pressure; in fact, many older men suffer unknowingly from the pride they share with their contemporaries. They seem to have a need to show they are not ashamed to use God's name in vain. But take a look at what the Savior has to say about this:

> You shall not take the name of the LORD your God
> in vain, for the LORD will not hold him guiltless

who takes His name in vain. (Exodus 20:7, the Third Commandment)

For whoever is ashamed of Me and My words in this adulterous and sinful generation, of him the Son of Man also will be ashamed when he comes in the glory of His Father with the holy angels. (Mark 8:38)

For whoever is ashamed of Me and My words, of him the Son of Man will be ashamed when He comes in His own glory, and in His Father's, and of the holy angels. (Luke 9:26)

For do I now persuade men, or God? Or do I seek to please men? For if I still pleased men, I would not be a bondservant of Christ. (Galatians 1:10)

Sixth, the calendar date by which this very *Considering Wisdom* was published is based on the birth of the Lord Jesus Christ. BC stands for "Before Christ," and AD refers to His incarnate birth. The letters AD stand for "Anno Domini," which is Latin for "The Year of our Lord," meaning the year of His coming down from heaven to dwell in the flesh with humankind. This is explained in the first chapter of the Gospel according to John.

In the beginning was the Word [Jesus], and the Word [Jesus] was with God [the Father in heaven], and the Word [Jesus] was God.... And the Word became flesh and dwelt among us, and we beheld His glory, the glory as of the only begotten of the Father, full of grace and truth. (John 1:1, 14)

"Begotten of the Father" means that God supernaturally caused the virgin woman Mary to conceive. Jesus is the only Son Whom the Father begot. He sent the Holy Spirit to the virgin to miraculously cause her to become pregnant.

That which is conceived in her is of the Holy Spirit.
(Matthew 1:20b)

The repetitions that occur in the Old Testament are followed by the four Gospel Books, which furthermore contain lots of duplication. Reiteration is also necessary in the continuation of clarifying how God's wisdom affects every aspect of our being. Due to diminishing family values, violence, rape, sexual immorality, schoolchildren killings, and gang murder rates—at all-time records in this world—we are approaching the same low level of wickedness that brought on God's destruction of the world in Genesis:

> Then the LORD saw that the wickedness of man was great in the earth, and that every intent of the thought of his heart was only evil continually. And the LORD was sorry that He had made man on the earth, and He was grieved in His heart. So the LORD said, "I will destroy man whom I have created from the face of the earth, both man and beast, creeping thing and birds of the air, for I am sorry that I have made them." (Genesis 6:5–7)

The result of God's fury was that only eight people survived: Noah, his wife, and their three sons with their wives. The ark that housed a male and female of each species of animal were also blessed to survive for the 150-day-long, life-saving event. God brought it all on by causing forty continuous days and nights of rain that flooded the earth.

Today, God promises to send His Son, the Lord Jesus Christ, to take all true believers up to meet Him in the air and to leave all unbelievers behind to suffer—like the victims of the flood, which was a foretaste of the upcoming Tribulation. This most certainly is not impossible for the intelligent designer of our earthly habitat and the entire universe that He created. The ones who will be left behind will be subjected to seven years of a most unimaginable tribulation that our all-powerful God will amass. If during the Great Tribulation, people cave in to the Antichrist and do not commit their lives to God, they will later be subjected to eternal suffering in the Lake of Fire, an unquenchable fire (Revelation 21:8). Much prayer needs to go up to God. The following prayer from 2 Chronicles chapter 7 would certainly be suitable for both our loved ones and for our nation:

> If My people who are called by My name will humble themselves, and pray and seek My face, and turn from their wicked ways, then I will hear from heaven, and will forgive their sin and heal their land.
> (2 Chronicles 7:14)

In the Bible, nations, cities, and individuals can draw a parallel. The immorality of a nation will cause its own demise, as the immorality of individuals will cause their own destruction. All surviving unbelievers will witness this downfall of nations and self.

> By the blessing of the upright the city is exalted, but it is overthrown by the mouth of the wicked.
> (Proverbs 11:11)

> Righteousness exalts a nation, but sin is a reproach to any people. (Proverbs 14:34)

There are certainly more than a couple of cities today that can be compared with Sodom and Gomorrah. God loves the people of these modern-day cities and does not want to see them perish:

> "Repent and turn from all your transgressions, so that iniquity [sin] will not be your ruin. Cast away from you all the transgressions which you have committed, and get yourselves a new heart and a new spirit. For why should you die?... For I have no pleasure in the death of one who dies," says the Lord GOD. "Therefore turn and live." (Ezekiel 18:30b-31a, 32)

God also loves politicians, and so do true believers. Neither this book nor this page would be written if our government officials weren't loved enough to inform them: For their own good, and to receive

God's blessings, presidents, administration officials, secretaries of state, and members of Congress should know what Almighty God says about diminishing support for Israel or their increased support for gay pride:

> I will bless those who bless you [Israel], and I will curse him who curses you; and in you all the families of the earth shall be blessed. (Genesis 12:3)

> God gave them up to vile passions. For even their women exchanged the natural use for what is against nature. Likewise also the men, leaving the natural use of the woman, burned in their lust for one another, men with men committing what is shameful, and receiving in themselves the penalty of their error which was due. And even as they did not like to retain God in their knowledge, God gave them over to a debased mind, to do those things which are not fitting. (Romans 1:26–28)

> Who, knowing the righteous judgment of God, that those who practice such things are deserving of death, not only do the same but also approve of those who practice them. (Romans 1:32)

> As Sodom and Gomorrah, and the cities around them in a similar manner to these, having given themselves over to sexual immorality and gone after strange flesh, are set forth as an example, suffering the vengeance of eternal fire. (Jude 7)

> Do you not know that the unrighteous will not inherit the kingdom of God? Do not be deceived. Neither fornicators, nor idolaters, nor adulterers, nor homosexuals, nor sodomites, nor thieves, nor covetous, nor drunkards, nor revilers, nor extortioners will inherit the kingdom of God. (1 Corinthians 6:9–10)

He who overcomes shall inherit all things [including heaven], and I will be his God and he shall be My son. But the cowardly, unbelieving, abominable, murderers, sexually immoral, sorcerers, idolaters, and all liars shall have their part in the lake which burns with fire and brimstone, which is the second death. (Revelation 21:7–8)

With deep, heartfelt sincerity, this is serious; it's truly a matter of life and death. This is the most crucial consideration a person can make during this temporary life here on earth. Eternity is a long, long time.

The time is near (Revelation 1:3b).

If a man lies with a male as he lies with a woman, both of them have committed an abomination. They shall surely be put to death. Their blood shall be upon them. (Leviticus 20:13)

I have publicly admitted that I was an adulterer. Since being saved, I no longer desire to live that lifestyle. This is shared to let all who may be practicing any of the above mentioned offenses know that what's being written is not hypocritical. It is also not hidden. This is pointed out so that whoever may hear this truth would repent and ask for forgiveness to receive the same blessings from our God that all believers experience. Believers have been set free from guilt and from the bondage of practicing sin.

Even though the Books of Leviticus and Revelation tell us the penalty for these offenses is death—that is, eternal suffering in the Lake of Fire—the Savior took the punishment for us by being hung on the cruel cross. He suffered and died for us.

But God demonstrates His own love toward us, in that while we were still sinners, Christ died for us. (Romans 5:8)

All these acts can be forgiven if we repent and ask God to forgive, even in a silent but sincere prayer:

> If we confess our sins, He is faithful and just to forgive us our sins and to cleanse us from all unrighteousness. (1 John 1:9)

This righteousness (God's view of us even though we are still sinners) is given to us simply by sincerely repenting and believing that Jesus is the Savior:

> But now the righteousness of God ... even the righteousness of God, through faith in Jesus Christ, to all and on all who believe. For there is no difference; for all have sinned and fall short of the glory of God. (Romans 3:21a, 22–23)

> For I will be merciful to their unrighteousness, and their sins and their lawless deeds I will remember no more." (Hebrews 8:12)

> For God so loved the world [not the planet, but the people] that He gave His only begotten Son, that whoever believes in Him should not perish but have everlasting life. For God did not send His Son into the world to condemn the world, but that the world through Him might be saved. (John 3:16–17)

For those who are lost, the only hope to be saved from eternal suffering is prayers to God. God will hear the prayers of those who are willing to listen and sincerely take His truth to heart. For nations and for individuals who sincerely turn around and go in the way that is pleasing to God, true repentance would result in hope for our nation, for our children, and for our grandchildren.

Some judges of the high courts have not been listening to what God says. They've made decisions with human schemes. Even the highest court in America, the Supreme Court of the United States, has had such differing and opposing judges. About half have ungodly, modern, rebellious leanings, and the other half leans towards God's ways and the original US Constitution.

In the Book of Acts, we see how God wants us to listen to Him and not to worldly advisors.

> But Peter and John answered and said to them, "Whether it is right in the sight of God to listen to you more than to God, you judge." (Acts 4:19)

> But Peter and the other apostles answered and said: "We ought to obey God rather than men." (Acts 5:29)

> For they loved the praise of men more than the praise of God. (John 12:43)

> It is better to trust in the Lord than to put confidence in man. (Psalm 118:8)

> [Jesus said,] "You are an offense to Me, for you are not mindful of the things of God, but the things of men." (Matthew 16:23b)

Oh, how we should pray that the judges are reading this and not only hearing but absorbing and consuming these Words of God.

> All Scripture is given by inspiration of God.
> (2 Timothy 3:16a)

> For do I now persuade men, or God? Or do I seek to please men? For if I still pleased men, I would not be a bondservant of Christ. (Galatians 1:10)

> And whatever you do, do it heartily, as to the Lord and not to men. (Colossians 3:23)

Danger in Resisting Authority

Most recently, we have seen many people resist the US president who won the election in 2016. God tells us that God Himself is the one who appoints the rulers of the nations. He does this by knowing our thoughts, our minds, and subsequently, some still have a foundation for thinking, and others have a debased mind and, hence, our votes. He is our Creator. He can do anything He pleases. Here's what He says about those who insist to resist:

> Let every soul be subject to the governing authorities. For there is no authority except from God, and the authorities that exist are appointed by God. Therefore whoever resists the authority resists the ordinance of God, and those who resist will bring judgment on themselves. (Romans 13:1–2)

Upon those who sin against God, vengeance is not for us to take:

> Vengeance is Mine, and recompense; their foot shall slip in due time; for the day of their calamity is at hand; and the things to come hasten upon them. (Deuteronomy 32:35)

> O LORD God, to whom vengeance belongs—O God, to whom vengeance belongs, shine forth! (Psalm 94:1)

> Your nakedness shall be uncovered, yes, your shame will be seen; I will take vengeance, and I will not arbitrate with a man. (Isaiah 47:3)

> For this is the day of the Lord GOD of hosts, a day of vengeance, that He may avenge Himself on His adversaries. (Jeremiah 46:10a)

Jesus says,

"For these are the days of vengeance, that all things which are written may be fulfilled" (Luke 21:22).

Beloved, do not avenge yourselves, but rather give place to wrath; for it is written, "Vengeance is Mine, I will repay," says the Lord. (Romans 12:19)

Journalists, politicians, resisters, judges: all will bow their knees with everyone else at judgment time. The following verses are well worth repeating:

For it is written [in Isaiah 45:23]: As I live, says the LORD, every knee shall bow to Me, and every tongue shall confess to God. (Romans 14:11)

That at the name of Jesus every knee should bow, of those in heaven, and of those on earth, and of those under the earth, and that every tongue should confess that Jesus Christ is Lord, to the glory of God the Father. (Philippians 2:10–11)

And there is no creature hidden from His sight, but all things are naked and open to the eyes of Him to whom we must give account. (Hebrews 4:13)

And I saw the dead, small and great, standing before God, and books were opened. And another book was opened, which is the Book of Life. And the dead were judged according to their works, by the things which were written in the books. The sea gave up the dead who were in it, and Death and Hādēs delivered up the dead who were in them. And they were judged, each one according to his works. Then Death and Hādēs were cast into the lake of fire. This is the second death. And anyone not found written in the Book of Life was cast into the lake of fire. (Revelation 20:12–15)

The Gospel according to Mark tells us five times that the fire shall never be quenched: Mark 9:43, 44, 45, 46, and 48.

When we reach the age of accountability, our consciences alert us when we commit an offensive act worthy of the above unimaginable punishment. We thank our God for saving the innocent children who have not yet discerned right from wrong.

Chapter 10
LUCIFER'S PROPAGANDA/ SPIRITUAL WARFARE

Our God and Savior, Jesus Christ, says,

> "Let the little children come to Me, and do not forbid them; for of such is the kingdom of God" (Luke 18:16b).

Children are on their way to heaven. However, when they reach the age of accountability—not exactly the same age for everyone—their journey is turned around, and unless they have come to believe in God, they are destined for the same place as all other nonbelievers. Unforgiven sinners are going toward the world instead of toward God. When they realize they are not right with God, and then come to believe in Him, sincerely regret their unrighteous actions, repent, and ask forgiveness, then they are forgiven and are on the right path to God's kingdom. Nothing can change God's plan.

God gives a stern warning:

> Then He [the Lord Jesus Christ] said to the disciples, "It is impossible that no offenses should come, but woe to him through whom they do come! It would be better for him if a millstone were hung around his neck, and he were thrown into the sea, than that he would offend one of these little ones." (Luke 17:1–2)

It is not our place to judge the unsaved of their sins. God does that judging. Nevertheless, it is our responsibility as parents and grandparents to give our love, concern, and care for our children and grandchildren. We love them so deeply that we fervently desire to love them and be with them from now on throughout all eternity.

> Train up a child in the way he should go, and when he is
> old he will not depart from it. (Proverbs 22:6)

Admittedly, if we're honest, some of us have done a very poor job with our sons and daughters, but we should desire to do better.

* * *

Again, the reason this truth of God's Word is shared is because of His love for all people. Having been led to a life-changing relationship with Jesus Christ, believers come to live a more guilt-free life with joy and hope for a glorious eternal future. Believers share God's desire for all to be saved and come to the knowledge of the truth:

> For this is good and acceptable in the sight of God our
> Savior, who desires all men to be saved and to come to
> the knowledge of the truth. (1 Timothy 2:3–4)

January 1993: The newly elected president's first official act was to change the policy in the US Armed Forces Uniform Code of Military Justice. The president's policy of "Don't Ask; Don't Tell" suddenly allowed homosexuals into the US military. Up until that time, the homosexual community kept much to themselves. Since that time, there's been a vast change: We've been seeing openly gay politicians, movie stars, television programs, and organized movements to bring awareness of the LGBTQ+ faction. From 1993 to 2018, the pace has gone from just touching the gas to full-throttle pedal to the metal. What an immense acceleration. Lucifer's propaganda is offending the little ones.

In both Canada and the United States, there's a huge difference of moral values between those who are believers in Christ and those who are not. Both nations have adopted customs and laws that directly oppose the natural laws of humankind—the laws of life that our Creator has put forth. God does not force Himself or His laws onto anyone; He simply offers a free invitation to His prescribed ways. Jesus says,

> So I say to you, ask, and it will be given to you; seek, and you will find; knock, and it will be opened to you. For everyone who asks receives, and he who seeks finds, and to him who knocks it will be opened. (Luke 11:9–10; Matthew 7:7–8)

> Then you will call upon Me and go and pray to Me, and I will listen to you. And you will seek Me and find Me, when you search for Me with all your heart. (Jeremiah 29:12–13)

> Seek Me and live.... Seek the LORD and live. (Amos 5:4b, 6a)

> Seek the LORD, all you meek of the earth, who have upheld His justice. Seek righteousness, seek humility. It may be that you will be hidden in the day of the LORD'S anger. (Zephaniah 2:3)

> I love those who love me, and those who seek me diligently will find me. (Proverbs 8:17)

Regardless of whether saved or unsaved, God still loves everyone. This includes both Democrats and Republicans, liberals and conservatives, and Canadians and Americans, for He loves everyone in the world. God's Word confirms that He is not biased:

> For God so loved the world that He gave His only begotten Son, that whoever believes in Him should not perish but have everlasting life. (John 3:16)

> For the LORD your God is God of gods and Lord of lords, the great God, mighty and awesome, who shows no partiality nor takes a bribe. (Deuteronomy 10:17)

> Then Peter opened his mouth and said: "In truth I perceive that God shows no partiality." (Acts 10:34)

> For there is no partiality with God. (Romans 2:11)

Paul the apostle wrote,

> But from those who seemed to be something—whatever they were, it makes no difference to me, God shows personal favoritism to no man—for those who seemed to be something added nothing to me. (Galatians 2:6).

It has been said, "It's ironic that as people become more liberal, they become less tolerant." Tolerance, diversity, and inclusiveness today omit God's teaching—the Bible—sound doctrine. And to be up-front about it, many liberal ethics conflict with and often disregard the values of God's Word and of believing families and individuals. The people with whom many liberals are being intolerant are Christians—Christians who are taught to respect the ones who're of different mindset:

> Let your gentleness be known to all men.
> (Philippians 4:5a).

Some time ago, the US Democrat Party changed their label from that of liberals to progressives, and more recently to Democratic Socialists. Their powerful agenda for globalization is spreading to other nations. The Book of Revelation reveals to us that in the end-times, there will be a one world government. "Globalism" has been added to the vocabulary. Nationalism (as well as Christianity) has been, is being, and will be contested, for the remainder of this Church Age. We are progressing toward the end-time.

One example of progressiveness is presently taking place in children's schools in British Columbia, Canada: An organization called Sexual Orientation and Gender Identity (SOGI)[42] is in cooperation with a foundation called Aware-Respect-Capacity (ARC) to go from early school to university level, indoctrinating children, even "little ones," as the Lord Jesus calls them—including five-year-olds in kindergarten.

The true believer is taught to have the same position on what offends God as God Himself holds: "Love the sinner, but not the sin." God the Father is quoted speaking to God the Son:

> "Your throne, O God, is forever and ever;… You have loved righteousness and hated lawlessness [sin]" (Hebrews 1:8b, 9a).

One of the primary motivators to allow SOGI teaching is that children who've wound up with homosexual couples are being bullied by other kids in the schools. The modern person probably does not understand that bullying does not only apply to the LGBTQ+ culture. Years ago, bullying was mainly done to kids who wore glasses, or who were bashful, or poor, or small, or overweight, or skinny, or any number of other reasons.

One of SOGI's main points is to stop the bullying in schools—which, on the surface, sounds good. True believers agree wholeheartedly. God's Word teaches to love one another. Having attended a SOGI parents' information meeting, this author felt the implication was that since Christian values are different, then the Christians must be the ones who are bullying. It needs to be pointed out: Simply because people say they are Christian does not mean they are. There are professed Christians who are not necessarily true believers in the God of Christianity. Stereotyping can bring about contentions. But again, the true Christian who is indwelt by the Holy Spirit can only be

---

[42] THE CHILLIWACK PROGRESS, "Parent finds SOGI resource lacking", February 6, 2018, (September 2019), https://www.theprogress.com/letters/parent-finds-sogi-resource-lacking/

understood by the commonality he has with other true Christians—
and believers do not desire to argue. They desire to love and tell the
truth.

> But avoid disputes, genealogies, contentions, and
> strivings about the law; for they are unprofitable and
> useless. (Titus 3:9)

As we continue toward the goal of mutual respect in a dialogue such
as this, a true believer humbly desires to be truly gentle and respectful.
Although we might disagree with the news outlets attempting to
indoctrinate minds with what each of us consider to be falsehoods
in our own opinion, the believer would rather not argue about it
and would allow others the freedom of their own opinions. True
Christians prefer to be indoctrinated by what they consider to be
sound doctrine—that is, God's Word, the Bible. When asked, they
are willing to share their thoughts and reasons for being who they
are. How can we eliminate the division that causes opposition and
argument in the first place?

> Do not correct a scoffer, lest he hate you; rebuke a wise
> man, and he will love you. (Proverbs 9:8)

> But avoid foolish and ignorant disputes, knowing that
> they generate strife. And a servant of the Lord must not
> quarrel but be gentle to all, able to teach, patient.
> (2 Timothy 2:23–24)

Strife is exertion or contention for superiority; a competition or contest
in a struggle for victory in opposing views. Division can be brought on
by anger, and if so, should be avoided.

> By pride comes nothing but strife, but with the well-
> advised is wisdom. (Proverbs 13:10)

> The beginning of strife is like releasing water; therefore
> stop contention before a quarrel starts. (Proverbs 17:14)

Believers value friendships and love for others too much to allow contentions to divide them. If our goal is to stop the already existing disagreements, then to eliminate division among ourselves, we should attempt to be of one accord—all in accordance with a common goal. We need to agree to live up to a standard. The standard should provide guidelines. What should the standard be? There is peace in unity. When people are all of one accord, they will be in agreement; they will all be of one mind; and there will be peace.

> Fulfill my joy by being likeminded, having the same love, being of one accord, of one mind. (Philippians 2:2)

> BEHOLD, how good and how pleasant it is for brethren to dwell together in unity! (Psalm 133:1)

Should the standard be dependent upon our wisdom or God's wisdom?

> But Peter and John answered and said to them, "Whether it is right in the sight of God to listen to you more than to God, you judge." (Acts 4:19)

> But Peter and the other apostles answered and said: "We ought to obey God rather than men." (Acts 5:29)

> It is better to trust in the LORD than to put confidence in man. (Psalm 118:8)

> Trust in the LORD with all your heart, and lean not on your own understanding. (Proverbs 3:5)

A believer "hears" God by what is in his conscience after reading what God had inspired the writers to include in the Bible—God's own Word:

> All Scripture is given by inspiration of God.
> (2 Timothy 3:16a)

The SOGI web page plays videos with soft background music to lure the listener with a persuasive campaign in an attempt to convey that what they are doing is all good.

> By smooth words and flattering speech deceive the hearts of the simple. (Romans 16:18b)

However, what is being taught tears down the foundation of marriage, as explained in the Scriptures.

> And the LORD God caused a deep sleep to fall on Adam, and he slept; and He took one of his ribs, and closed up the flesh in its place. Then the rib which the LORD God had taken from man He made into a woman, and He brought her to the man. And Adam said: "This is now bone of my bones and flesh of my flesh; she shall be called Woman, because she was taken out of Man." Therefore a man shall leave his father and mother and be joined to his wife, and they shall become one flesh. (Genesis 2:21–24)

> A bishop [overseer or elder] then must be the husband of one wife. (1 Timothy 3:2a)

> Let deacons be the husbands of one wife, ruling their children and their own houses well. (1 Timothy 3:12)

The New Testament concept of one man being married to one woman is analogous with One God and Savior being married to His church—the church being made up of all believers. The Lord Jesus is the Groom of His betrothed church. God separates all sin from Himself. He wants His bride to be pure. He does not classify any of the information in the Bible as being confidential, secret, or top secret. He advocates for high standards in family values. He explains in full and hides nothing.

The very first question that was asked in the Bible:

> "Has God indeed said?" (Genesis 3:1b)

Who asked that question?

It was Satan himself. Perhaps one may be asking the same question in regard to whether or not God detests what the LGBTQ+ movement is doing: "Has God indeed said...?"

> Then the LORD spoke... "You shall not lie with a male
> as with a woman. It is an abomination."
> (Leviticus 18:1a, 22)

To God, when He says "it is an abomination," it means it is detestable behavior." The Gay Pride Parade participants should look deeply into what exactly is being declared. The definition of pride: "inordinate self-esteem; an unreasonable conceit of one's own superiority... which reveals itself in lofty airs, distance, reserve; often in contempt of others; insolence; rude treatment of others; that which excites boasting."[43]

The letter "T" in LGBTQ+ most likely stands for either transgender or transvestite—or both. In any case, it goes against what our Maker has designed. The Spirit of God is trying to inform all of the souls represented in these LGBTQ+ letters. For example, the transvestite should heed this warning:

> A woman shall not wear anything that pertains to a
> man, nor shall a man put on a woman's garment, for all
> who do so are an abomination to the LORD your God.
> (Deuteronomy 22:5)

Because every human being has Adam's DNA, we are all born with the nature to disobey God—that is, to commit sin. The opposition to God declares it to be fact that homosexuals are "born that way." This sets precedence for a pedophile—that is, one desiring to have sex with small children—to say, "It just couldn't be helped," while claiming, also, to be "born that way"—victimized. The pedophile-excuse of being born

---

[43] The original *American Dictionary of the English Language*, Noah Webster, 1828, s.v. "pride"

that way could furthermore be applied to a rapist. Should there be a "Pedophile Pride Parade" or, perhaps, an "Adulterer's Pride Parade" or a "Thief's Pride Parade" or a "Liar's Pride Parade"?

All these abominations to God carry the same penalty at the Great White Throne Judgment: it's called the "second death," which translates to the eternal conscious suffering in the Lake of Fire:

> But the cowardly, unbelieving, abominable, murderers, sexually immoral, sorcerers, idolaters, and all liars shall have their part in the lake which burns with fire and brimstone, which is the second death. (Revelation 21:8)

The obvious contrast is that believers in Christ are not proud of their offensive sins; rather, the Christian is ashamed and remorseful. That's the reason true believers bring it out into the light by confessing, repenting, and asking for forgiveness, and they are then set free of their guilt. Only by the help of the indwelling Spirit can we stop practicing our previous lifestyle. And we can only receive the Spirit if we first sincerely repent, ask forgiveness, and believe in the truth that the Savior, Jesus Christ, is the Son of the Living Father God Who, through the Holy Spirit, raised Jesus from the dead.

Exchanging God's natural laws of procreation causes a spiraling-down effect to arrive at violence, and eventually all the way to murderers, serial killers, and mass executioners; a truth worth repeating, especially with the topic being discussed:

> For this reason God gave them up to vile passions. For even their women exchanged the natural use for what is against nature. Likewise also the men, leaving the natural use of the woman, burned in their lust for one another, men with men committing what is shameful, and receiving in themselves the penalty of their error which was due. And even as they did not like to retain God in their knowledge, God gave them over to a debased mind, to do those things which are

not fitting; being filled with all unrighteousness, sexual immorality, wickedness, covetousness, maliciousness full of envy, murder, strife, deceit, evil-mindedness; they are whisperers [gossipers]. (Romans 1:26–29)

The bad news God gives us is that we were all born with Adam's DNA and his nature to sin. We can all be tempted to stray away from being pleasing to God. But the good news He gives us if we believe in God: The Father sent His Son the Savior to take the penalty of death in our place, and to forgive us by shedding His blood. On the third day, the Father, through the Spirit, raised Jesus from the dead. Upon believing this, we then have the help of God's indwelling Spirit to keep us on God's desired path.

> No temptation has overtaken you except such as is common to man; but God is faithful [to those who believe in Him], who will not allow you to be tempted beyond what you are able, but with the temptation will also make the way of escape, that you may be able to bear it. (1 Corinthians 10:13)

What are these temptations? The ARC Foundation has three tempting goals: Awareness, Respect, and Capacity. The first goal is to make the general population (including children) aware of the issues of the disenfranchised (slaves or bondservants) and the impact of prejudices. A kindhearted person could be tempted to have compassion and go along with this invitation.

This first goal of bringing about awareness of the impact of prejudices raises the question, "Who is prejudiced?" The definition of being prejudice is "to prepossess with unexamined opinions, or opinions formed without due knowledge of the facts and circumstances attending the question; to bias the mind by hasty and incorrect notions, and give it an unreasonable bent to one side or other of a cause. In short: Prepossessed by unexamined opinions; biased."[44]

---

[44] The original *American Dictionary of the English Language*, Noah Webster, 1828, s.v. "prejudice"

Webster's Dictionary goes on to explain the results of being prejudicial: "hurtful, mischievous; injurious; disadvantageous; detrimental, tending to obstruct or impair." Again, this necessitates the same question: "Who is prejudiced?" If a Christian family has strong faith and belief in God and desires to bring up their children in the way the family desires, should any public organization attempt to sway their children to a different set of values? Wouldn't it be prejudicial to indoctrinate those children with a belief system that opposes the family's values and beliefs? True believers, who know they were also sinful offenders to God, do not attempt to force their belief upon others. Only God can judge the sinner. No one can take God's place in this judgment. However, if the situation arises in a conversation, the believer will share the truth:

> God our Savior, who desires all to be saved and come to
> the knowledge of the truth. (1Timothy 2:3b-4)

Believers only want to share the joy of knowing they have been forgiven and set free and no longer have to feel guilty, and they have something other religions don't have: hope. Quoting Pat Boone: "That's the thing about atheism: it doesn't take away the pain. It only takes away the hope."[45]

Our Lord and God says,

> "Repent, and turn from all your transgressions, so that
> iniquity will not be your ruin.… For I have no pleasure
> in the death of one who dies," says the LORD GOD.
> "Therefore turn and live!" (Ezekiel 18:30b, 32)

Believers share this desire with God for no one to suffer torment. That's the very reason for this writing: to inform whomever may be reading. You are loved with godly love.

The second ARC goal is to create an environment of respect for the disenfranchised [slaves or bondservants] and marginalized through

---

[45]   *God's Not Dead 2,* directed by Harold Cronk, (2016, Pure Flix Entertainment, Scottsdale, Arizona) DVD, line by Pat Boone, (June 2019)

education. The true believing Christian is taught to treat others with kindness and respect.

> Honor all people. (1 Peter 2:17a)

> Always be ready to give a defense to everyone who asks you a reason for the hope that is in you, with meekness and fear [respect]. (1 Peter 3:15b)

And what is the "hope that is in you"? It is the hope for eternal life after death, and believers hope that for everyone.

> For this is the will of God, that by doing good you may put to silence the ignorance of foolish men.
> (1 Peter 2:15)

True Christians only want to help by showing love and respect ... and by sharing God's truth.

If Christians are being bullied for their beliefs, wouldn't it be intolerant and disrespectful on the part of the nonbelievers? But we don't hear of the true believer complaining about it, because it is expected. The Lord Jesus Himself told all believers:

> "If they persecuted Me, they will also persecute you."
> (John 15:20b)

Is it actually hurting anyone if people who believe in God bow their heads and pray for safety before a football game? Isn't it bullying to force Christians to be silenced?

The third ARC goal is to develop capacity within those less tolerant for understanding and acceptance. Understanding is not difficult for a true believer, because we have all been there—with whatever offenses to God and other people we may have committed. These offenses are called sins. So the solid believer is only capable of making others aware by showing respect and love of the sinner, but not openly accepting the offense. The offense grieves God and grieves the indwelling Holy Spirit within the believer.

Since the progressive, liberal party advocates tolerance, it seems extremely intolerant to sue believers for wanting to keep their Christian values. If a bakery owner happens to be a believer in God, wouldn't it make good sense for same-sex couples—who want a cake with a same-gender figurine—not to press the issue to the point of the business being shut down? Why couldn't the couple be tolerant and go to a different bakery?

The sincere, genuine Christian really would be faced with a dilemma by being tolerant and approving of offensive, sinful acts. Here's the reason:

> "who, knowing the righteous judgment of God, that those who practice such things are deserving of death, not only do the same but also approve of those who practice them." (Romans 1:32)

From June 26 to August 21, 2017, the prime minister of Canada participated in three Gay Pride Parades in Montreal, Halifax, and Toronto. He marched along on the street waving a rainbow flag. This fulfills the above verse by directly approving those who practice these sins. True believers are praying for the prime minister's soul—for him to turn around, to repent, and to be saved. He should remember that he represents others besides the LGBTQ+ movement who are also paying his wages.

The deep, reverent respect Christians have for God keeps them from falling for such and has them withdraw from such.

> Now I urge you brethren, note those who cause divisions and offenses, contrary to the doctrine which you learned and avoid them. (Romans 16:17)

Christian married couples do not want their private bedroom activities publicly made known. To them, it's nobody else's business. This is a deeply personal, intimate sharing of affection that is kept respectful within the marriage relationship. A Christian wife or husband does not want the spouse to be telling others what is so very special and is not to be shared with anyone else. This shows respect for one's spouse. God's sacred Word even gives instruction for a married couple to provide the affection which the spouse deserves.

> Let the husband render to his wife the affection due her, and likewise also the wife to her husband.
> (1 Corinthians 7:3)

> But he who is married cares about the things of the world—how he may please his wife. (1 Corinthians 7:33)

> But she who is married cares about the things of the world—how she may please her husband.
> (1 Corinthians 7:34b)

> So God created man in His own image, in the image of God He created him; male and female He created them. Then God blessed them, and God said to them, "Be fruitful and multiply" (Genesis 1:27–28a)

> He created them male and female, and blessed them and called them Mankind in the day they were created. (Genesis 5:2)

> And every living thing of all flesh you shall bring two of every sort into the ark, to keep them alive with you; they shall be male and female. (Genesis 6:19)

> And He [Jesus] answered and said to them, "Have you not read that He who made them at the beginning 'made them male and female,' and said, 'For this reason a man shall leave his father and mother and be joined to his wife, and the two shall become one flesh'? So then they are no longer two but one flesh. Therefore what God has joined together, let not man separate." (Matthew 19:4–6)

But from the beginning of the creation, God "made them male and female." (Mark 10:6)

By producing male and female hormones, God created the sexual drive that results in procreation. And He also teaches us not to deprive one another for too long a period of time so that lack of self-control will not yield to the world's vast array of temptations.

> Do not deprive one another except with consent for a time, that you may give yourselves to fasting and prayer [devote yourself to giving attention to the Lord during the greater time when you are not devoting yourself to the shorter times of fulfilling your spouse's desires]; and come together again [satisfying sexual affection with your spouse] so that Satan does not tempt you because of your lack of self-control. (1 Corinthians 7:5)

We see then that "God addresses human sexuality from a gentle, respectful perspective of God's own intention and design. He does this with tenderness and without vulgarity. In contrast to modern day increasingly compelling obsession with sex, the Bible places sex within the total context of human nature, happiness, and holiness."[46]

Married Christians are taught to conduct their daily walk in life in the way that pleases God and their spouse.

> Finally then, brethren, we [the apostles] urge and exhort in the Lord Jesus that you should abound more and more, just as you received from us how you ought to walk and to please God. (1 Thessalonians 4:2)

The single Christians are also taught to please God:

> He who is unmarried cares—how he may please the Lord. (1 Corinthians 7:32b)

---

[46] *Holman Illustrated Bible Dictionary,* (Holman Bible Publishers, 2003) pg 1469, s.v. "sex"

Christians have no desire to know what another person does in their own bedroom. The stark contrast here is that God does not force Himself onto anyone, but the LGBTQ+ movement wants to put this indoctrination upon everyone, including five-year-olds. Sexual activity is private and not for other people to know, saved or unsaved. No one else needs to be aware of it. But know this: Our omniscient God knows (Psalm 139:1–6). The Christian loves them and tells them the truth, but leaves the judging up to God.

Whenever an "in-your-face" approach is attempted by a professed Christian to preach God's Word, it is an affront to those who have not been taught. Likewise, whenever an in-your-face approach is made to indoctrinate believers with something that is not agreeable with Christian doctrine, it is disrespectful to the believers.

With SOGI and ARC manipulation and indoctrination of children's minds, confusion can arise for the young people who are being raised in Christian environments. Are not the parents (who might have thus far raised their children to live by God's standards) and their children becoming the real victims of this abusive indoctrination of their offspring?

It's been suggested by some that if Christian parents don't want their children to attend the SOGI and ARC sessions held at the schools, then it's not required. There are at least three problems with this proposal: First, these scheduled meetings are often held on short notice. Second, the kindergarten-aged children are expected to carry a note home to their parents and remember to give it to them. Third, not all children have Christian parents who care about their eternal futures. Who is to decide which doctrine is right for them? If Bible teaching is not allowed in school, but SOGI is, then is it fair?

Adults are also affected: If educational and government officials deem something like SOGI to be acceptable, then, in the minds of many, it must be okay. Whether it is a pornographic shop or an adult theater on Main Street, a gambling casino, multi-gender curriculum, use of recreational drugs, or violent games on social media, if it is approved by city, state, and federal officials, then it must be okay. But is it?

SOGI publishes "Three Essentials for Their Inclusive Schools." First, they say that their policies and procedures have proven to reduce discrimination, suicidal ideation, and suicide attempts for all students. However, there were no statistics publicly available on the internet to back the claim of reduced suicidal ideation. *Statistics Canada* affirms, "Among those aged 15–34, suicide was the second leading cause of death, preceded only by accidents (unintentional deaths)."[47] The US National Library of Medicine National Institutes of Health claims in "Can We Really Prevent Suicide?" that "the suicide rate increases with age, although suicide rates among young people have been increasing to such an extent that they are now the group at highest risk in a third of countries, in both developed and developing countries."[48] Mental disorders (particularly depression and alcohol use disorders) are a major risk factor. The publication *Christianity Today* reports that in the United States, "In 2015, more than 44,000 Americans died by suicide—one death every 12 minutes, as the Department of Health and Human Services put it. The overall suicide rate has grown by nearly 30 percent over the past 15 years."[49] It would be difficult to deny that not only have sexual immoral acts increased dramatically in the past fifteen years, but public promotion and indoctrination of such acts has also increased.

According to Romans 1:18–32, there is likely a correlation. Verse 28 in this passage:

> And even as they did not like to retain God in their knowledge, God gave them over to a debased mind, to do those things which are not fitting. (Romans 1:28)

---

[47] Statistics Canada, Health at a Glance, "Suicide rates: An Overview", Tanya Navaneelan, #Suicide is a leading cause of death in young people, last sentence in 1st paragraph (June 2019) https://www150.statcan.gc.ca/n1/pub/82-624-x/2012001/article/11696-eng.htm

[48] NCBI, PMC34922539, 1 Dec. 2013, "Can We Really Prevent Suicide?", #Introduction 7th sentence, (June 2019) https://www.ncbi.nlm.nih.gov/pmc/articles/PMC3492539/

[49] CHRISTIANITY TODAY, The CT Interview, "The Truth About Suicide", Morgan Lee, October 20, 2017, 1st paragraph, (June 2019) https://www.christianitytoday.com/ct/2017/november/suicide-americans-taking-their-own-lives-church-al-hsu.html

With a "debased mind," when there is no base—that is, no foundation—the mind not being grounded with God's ways for discerning how to make the best decisions, then the Lord turns the mind over to having no base point, a lack of reasoning ability.

According to the *Mental Health Commission of Canada,* "The evidence is also clear that mental illness, depression in particular, is the most significant risk factor for suicide."[50] Concluding that when the mind becomes depressed, then suicide risk is heightened.

SOGI's second essential for inclusive schools is that "inclusive learning environments—including SOGI and LGBTQ+ signage, word choices, and extracurricular opportunities—create a positive and welcoming space for all students." Comparing the LGBTQ+ movement to the Christian environment, God's Word gives this truth:

> Do you not know that the unrighteous will not inherit the kingdom of God? Neither fornicators, nor idolaters, nor adulterers, nor homosexuals, nor sodomites, nor thieves, nor covetous, nor drunkards, nor revilers, nor extortioners will inherit the kingdom of God.
> (1 Corinthians 6:9–10)

> He who overcomes shall inherit all things, and I will be his God and he shall be My son [or daughter]. But the cowardly, unbelieving, abominable, murderers, sexually immoral, sorcerers, idolaters, and all liars shall have their part in the lake which burns with fire and brimstone, which is the second death.
> (Revelation 21:7–8)

SOGI's third essential for inclusive schools is "to teach that diversity and respect that include examples of SOGI topics and LGBTQ+ community

---

[50] Mental Health Commission of Canada, December 2018, "Research on Suicide and its Prevention", #III Summary Report, 2nd paragraph 1st sentence, (June 2019) https://www.mentalhealthcommission.ca/sites/default/files/2018-12/Research_on_suicide_prevention_dec_2018_eng.pdf

members allow learning to reflect the SOGI diversity in students' lives and society."

Jesus is alive in heaven, awaiting His Father's command to descend to the air and take up His Church. This soon-coming event is called the Rapture. Jesus is the head of the body, which is also alive. A live head must have a live body. God's Word speaks of diversity in this way: He teaches that there is diversity in the gifts He bestows upon His unified body of believers so that He is represented to the unbelievers by a living organism with total dispersion and truth of who He is.

> And He Himself gave some to be apostles, some prophets, some evangelists, and some pastors and teachers, for the equipping of the saints for the work of ministry, for the edifying of the body of Christ, till we all come to the unity of the faith and of the knowledge of the Son of God, to a perfect man, to the measure of the stature of the fullness of Christ that we should no longer be children, tossed to and fro and carried about with every wind of doctrine, by the trickery of men, in the cunning craftiness of deceitful plotting, but, speaking the truth in love, may grow up in all things into Him who is the head—Christ—from whom the whole body, joined and knit together by what every joint supplies, according to the effective working by which every part does its share, causes growth of the body for the edifying of itself in love. (Ephesians 4:11–16)

In short, God's diversity is not a variety of values and interpretations, but rather diversity of gifts to exercise and serve Him.

* * *

One of the biggest shock waves in history occurred in when a tsunami suddenly struck several nations bordering the Indian Ocean. A cable news program—*Hannity and Colmes*—had a discussion concerning the tsunami that involved Franklin Graham, Billy Graham's son.

Alan Colmes asked Graham, "If God is such a loving God, why did He allow such a tragedy to instantly take the lives of so many people?"

Mr. Graham paused and replied, "When those people were on the beach, rubbing their suntan lotion onto their bodies, they weren't expecting such a catastrophic thing to happen. I just hope they were prepared to meet God." He paused. "Are you prepared, Mr. Colmes?"

Alan Colmes died on February 23, 2017. I sincerely hope that he was prepared.

Every morning when we wake up, we are one day closer to either our death or the Rapture. We never know the day or hour of the end of our earthly lives. The invitation to live for all eternity is "a positive and welcoming" message from the God Who, in the same Book, also gives warnings about not listening to Him:

> "Prepare to meet your God!" (Amos 4:12b)

Tragic events and natural deaths of loved ones both bring the ultimate change to life's past routines. God's Word cautions us to be vigilant and to look ahead to something much more important than this brief earthly life.

> Forgetting those things which are behind and reaching forward to those things which are ahead. (Colossians 3:2)

> Set your mind on things above, not on things on the earth. (Philippians 3:13b)

> Do not lay up for yourselves treasures on earth, where moth and rust destroy and where thieves break in and steal; but lay up for yourselves treasures in heaven, where neither moth nor rust destroys and where thieves do not break in and steal. For where your treasure is, there your heart will be also. (Matthew 6:19–21)

Be prepared. Look ahead. Be ready for eternity.

Christians have difficulties in life's trials, just like everyone else, but having such loving, believing brothers and sisters in Christ for support and encouragement, and having a comforting God to lean on in times of mourning, provides a flow of love that surpasses all understanding.

> And the peace of God, which surpasses all understanding, will guard your hearts and minds through Christ Jesus. (Philippians 4:7)

> Blessed be the God and Father of our Lord Jesus Christ, the Father of mercies and God of all comfort, who comforts us in all our tribulation, that we may be able to comfort those who are in any trouble, with the comfort with which we ourselves are comforted by God. (2 Corinthians 1:3–4)

As we see from Scripture, God's comfort is part of His doctrine. If His doctrine—that is, His teaching—is not taught, then children, who aren't blessed to have access to God's Word elsewhere are denied the privilege of acquiring His full comfort.

World religions are taught in some colleges and universities. However, Bibles are not allowed to be used on government property nor for teaching in most state-run K–12 schools. If the doctrine of religions can be taught, it would make sense if the students could compare the key writings of Christianity to all the other religions. It would provide a more thorough education and would be fair to all.

DELICATE ISSUE

Life is in the blood. (Leviticus 17:11)

Jesus said,

"Let the little children come to Me." (Mark 10:14b)

Everything in *Considering Wisdom* is written solely for the glory of God. This upcoming subject is no exception. The matter is so delicate that one must exercise extreme concern for emotional feelings when bringing forth this line of reasoning. Since this chapter's topic is abortion, it requires extreme, caring love to explain.

Although abortion is sensitive to discuss, should we not accept the reality of its taking place?

Without doubt, we need to be sensitive with people who have had an abortion, or who've been involved with an abortion, or may have loved ones in their family who have experienced one. Not knowing whether a person supports abortion rights or not, this calls for utmost sensitivity and prayer that this chapter will at least provide encouragement and instill some lasting thoughts and considerations.

Since abortion is an issue that not everyone agrees upon, what will be brought forth is not meant to incite argument. What will be found is information that might not have previously been introduced or explained. It is presented with respect and no attempt to rob anyone of dignity. The opposing sides seem to be motivated by bias from both society and the media, and by God's Word. Society and the media use the wisdom of men. For example:

Indoctrinated by society, some women have been motivated to be more concerned about their respect being stripped away than got regard of how their futures can be affected. The sympathy they feel they deserve is out of decency for their constitutional right to choose.

As followers of the Lord Jesus Christ, believers desire to be considerate of others, but most importantly, our God provides clear instructions for all matters—including abortion. Jane Roe, who'd gotten pregnant with an unwanted third child in 1969, was the person who took the legality question to court.

On January 22, 1973, the US Supreme Court ruled 7–2 that a woman's decision to have an abortion was protected by the "due process" clause of the Constitution's Fourteenth Amendment for her right to privacy. The Court later rejected *Roe*'s trimester framework, easing the restriction for a woman's right to abortion until viability of the fetus. Viability is described in the *Roe* decision as "the point in time that a fetus can potentially sustain its own life without the support of the mother—outside the mother's womb, albeit with artificial aid," adding that viability "is usually placed at about seven months (28 weeks) but may occur earlier, even at 24 weeks." The court's definition of viability raises the question: "Can a one-week-old baby support itself outside the mother's womb without assistance?" How about a five-month-old—or a two-year-old?

Considering viability, baby fawns are protected from being hunted up until the June-born fawn is able to support itself without the mother's help. In the Canadian Kootenay hunting Regions 4-1 to 4-9, 4-14 to 4-40, the doe cannot be hunted until the nursing period ends four months later, in October.[51] Comparing this regulation to laws governing human beings' viability begs for wisdom to be considered.

There was so much confusion after the *Roe* decision that all kinds of laws were passed in favor of the right to choose, but then many laws were drastically changed or done away with completely:

Controversial state laws were passed to require parental consent for minors to obtain abortions, parental notification laws, spousal mutual consent laws, spousal notification laws, laws requiring abortions to be performed in hospitals but not clinics, laws barring state funding for abortions, laws banning intact dilation and extraction (also known as partial-birth abortion), and laws requiring waiting periods before abortion. But most of these laws have either been struck down or have been fought with fierce battles by those who continue to support abortion.

Some of the opposing pro-life advocates have gone too far by violently attacking abortion clinics and by being downright rude to the pro-choice people. On the other hand, many have offered a different kind of choice:

ABORTION
D P

Perhaps the most notable opposition to *Roe* comes from Norma L. McCorvey (alias Jane Roe), who admitted in 1995—twenty-two years after the court's decision—that she had become pro-life and was now, herself, a vocal opponent of abortion and the *Roe* decision.

Some subjects have become difficult to discuss because of our culture's demand for political correctness. Should any part of God's Word be squelched because of pressure from our society? Do cultures change God, or does God change cultures? Should we rely upon the wisdom of men who are in judge's robes? According to some past judges and

---

[51] British Columbia 2018–2020 Hunting and Trapping Regulations and Synopsis, Effective July 1, 2018 to June 30, 2020, pg 50

today's politicians, life does not begin until a baby takes its first breath of air after the umbilical cord is cut from the mother's support system. Recently, some have even gone beyond to say a decision of whether the baby will live or die can be made after the baby who survives a botched abortion is actually born.

> The foolishness of God is wiser than men.
> (1 Corinthians 1:25a)

> Let no one deceive himself. If anyone among you seems to be wise in this age, let him become a fool that he may become wise. For the wisdom of this world is foolishness with God. For it is written, "He catches the wise in their own craftiness" [Job 5:13]; and again, "The LORD knows the thoughts of the wise, that they are futile." [Psalm 94:11] (1 Corinthians 3:18–20)

So what we learn from God's Word is that we should seriously consider the decisions of judges with a great measure of discernment.

Further in God's Word, we learn that we should listen to our Lord rather than men:

> We ought to obey God rather than men. (Acts 5:29b)

What does God say about life?

> For the life of the flesh [a creature] is in the blood.
> (Leviticus 17:11a)

Those who've had first-aid training have learned the first step to save a life is to stop the bleeding.

According to Héma-Québec, "A drop of blood the size of a pinhead contains approximately 5 million red blood cells (erythrocytes)."[52]

---

52   HEMA QUEBEC (2014-2019), "BLOOD" #Red Blood Cells, 1st sentence, (December 2019) https://www.hema-quebec.qc.ca/sang/savoir-plus/composants.en.html

On December 2010, the *Calgary CTV News* agreed with what God says (in more ways than one), saying, "Blood is the gift of life."[53]

Red blood cells give blood its red color. They also carry oxygen from the lungs to the body's organs and tissues and take carbon dioxide back to the lungs to be exhaled.

Plasma is the liquid portion of blood. Plasma transports water and nutrients to the body's tissues. According to *Dorland's Pocket Medical Dictionary 27th Edition*, "blood—the fluid circulating through the heart, arteries, capillaries, and veins, carrying nutriment and oxygen to body cells, and removing waste products and carbon dioxide. It consist of the liquid portion (the plasma) and the formed elements (erythrocytes, leukocytes, and platelets)."[54] "Plasma also contains proteins which defend our bodies against invaders and help blood to clot."[55] Validated shipping containers are critical to the transportation of blood which is to be used for transfusions. These containers are necessary to ensure blood components remain within environmental specifications at all times, to maintain the blood's anticoagulation, preservative, life-support capability, to keep the blood itself "alive."

"Containers and coolant packs used for this purpose are required to reduce the temperature of freshly donated blood from body temperature (+37°C) to +22°C ± 2°C within 4 hours of collection. After this initial cooling, requiring considerable heat to be transferred to the coolant pack, the container is expected to maintain the temperature within that range for up to 24 hours."[56]

---

[53] CTV News, Calgary December 4, 2010, "Santa gives the gift of life", 3rd paragraph, (December 2019) https://calgary.ctvnews.ca/santa-gives-the-gift-of-life-1.582287

[54] Dorland's Pocket Medical Dictionary, (Elsevier Saunders, 2004), pg 121, s.v. "blood"

[55] Australian Academy of Science, People & Medicine, "Plasma, the liquid gold running through our veins", Dr. Janet Wong MBBS FRCPA, Dr. Peta Dennington, #Essentials – 3rd paragraph (December 2019), https://www.science.org.au/curious/people-medicine/plasma

[56] Wiley Online Library, ISBT Science Series, "Blood Storage and Transportation", J. Hardwick, 09 May 2008, #Transportation of fresh blood from collection area to processing centre, 1st paragraph, (December 2019) https://onlinelibrary.wiley.com/doi/full/10.1111/j.1751-2824.2008.00196.x

"Plasma is the largest part of your blood. It, makes up more than half (about 55%) of its overall content. When separated from the rest of the blood, plasma is a light yellow liquid. Plasma carries water, salts and enzymes."[57]

"Semen, also called seminal fluid, fluid that is emitted from the male reproductive tract and that contains sperm cells, which are capable of fertilizing the female eggs. Semen also contains other liquids, known as seminal plasma, which help to keep the sperm cells viable.... Fluids contributed by the seminal vesicles are approximately 60 percent of the total semen volume."[58]

"Semen needs to be kept close to body temperature from the time collected until delivered. Sperm can die quickly at colder or warmer temperatures. If the cup is being transported during winter months, the best thing to do is to keep it close to your body temperature. You need to make sure it's just about body temperature, anything well above or below increases the risk of too many sperm dying."[59]

Sperm are reproductive cells in semen that have a head and a tail. Each sperm contains one copy of each chromosome (that is, all of the male's genes). Sperm are motile, normally moving forward through the semen. Inside a woman's body, this property enables them to travel to and fuse with the female's egg, resulting in fertilization—that is, conception. At this point, life has been transferred due to the viability of the male sperm and the female egg.

"Upon reaching an egg, enzymes contained within the sperm acrosome are activated, enabling the sperm to traverse the thick coat surrounding

[57] University of Rochester Medical Center, Health Encyclopedia, What is Plasma, "Facts about Plasma", (December 2019) https://www.urmc.rochester.edu/encyclopedia/content.aspx?ContentTypeID=160&ContentID=37

[58] ENCYCLOPEDIA BRITANNICA, "Semen" Biochemistry, May 27, 2020, 1st and 3rd paragraph, (May 2020) https://www.britannica.com/science/semen

[59] babyMed, Infertility, IVF, "How to Transport Semen for IVF?", Amos Grünebaum, November 15, 2018, #Transporting the Semen Specimen, 1st paragraph, (June 2019) https://www.babymed.com/ivf/how-transport-semen-vitro-fertilization-or-intrauterine-insemination

the egg (the zona pellucida); this process is known as the acrosome reaction. The membrane of the sperm cell then fuses with that of the egg, and the sperm nucleus is conveyed into the egg."[60]

In *Webster's Dictionary*, *lifeblood* is defined as the blood necessary to life; vital blood; that which is essential to existence or strength.[61]

Having just read in Leviticus 17:11 that "the life of the flesh [a creature] is in the blood," God's Word repeats it twice more three verses later:

> For it is the life of all flesh [every creature]. Its blood sustains its life. (Leviticus 17:14a)

> For the life of all flesh [every creature] is its blood. (Leviticus 17:14c)

Human life goes through phases: the embryo stage, the fetal stage, birth, infancy, toddler, teen, and adult life. *Embryo* is defined in *Webster's Dictionary* as "the beginning or first state of anything." So in this case, the embryo is the beginning of human life.

Murder is defined in the same dictionary: "to kill (a human being) with premeditated malice." And in the *Holman Illustrated Bible Dictionary*, *murder* is defined as the "intentional taking of human life."[62]

The definition is not limited to any particular stage of human life. It simply states that "murder is the intentional taking of human life." God clearly orders us not to murder in the fifth of the Ten Commandments: And God spoke...

> "You shall not murder."
> (Exodus 20:1a, 13; Deuteronomy 5:17)

---

[60] ENCYCLOPEDIA BRITANNICA, "SPERM" Physiology, 5th paragraph, (June 2019) https://www.britannica.com/science/sperm

[61] *The New Webster Encyclopedic Dictionary of the English Language*, (Consolidated Book Publishers Chicago, Processing & Books, Inc), s.v. "lifeblood"

[62] *Holman Illustrated Bible Dictionary* (Holman Bible Publishers, 2003) pg 1158, s.v. "murder"

Essentially, judges have decided that it is okay to take human life; that is, to murder.

When Peter and John the apostles were commanded not to speak at all nor teach in the name of Jesus, they answered:

> Whether it is right in the sight of God to listen to you
> [men] more than to God, you judge. (Acts 4:19b)

Prematurely disconnecting the umbilical between the fetus and the mother stops the blood flow and results in the death of the fetus. Life's opposition is death. That is, the opposite of life is death. Fetal heartbeats have been detected as early as six weeks.

Realizing this fundamental truth requires an in-depth look into when the fetus actually acquired the state of first becoming a living being. Human life is transferred to the next generation by the parents. If the father does not have life-living plasma in his sperm (unless using artificial insemination—that is, with life-giving plasma), the next generation cannot begin to live.

Life is transferred at conception. Children often look like one of their parents. This then raises the next question, "How does heredity of genes take place?" In 1973, the judges did not know much about DNA.

DNA is the source of heredity itself. The parents' DNA is mixed together in the fluid of the semen and the ovum (the egg) upon conception, when they together form a seed. Upon this impregnation, the seed develops into an embryo and continues to grow and become a fetus. The fetus stage continues to the development of the baby. After delivery, the baby continues to mature toward puberty and eventually becomes an adult. Each step of the living being is essential for developing to maturity. If one of the early phases (i.e., embryo, fetus, baby, child, or teen) of development is interrupted by death, then, of course, adulthood would not be achieved.

The DNA reveals the secret of transferred life. DNA provides and confirms the continuity of parental life. The baby is forever in the bloodline of the parents. Blood, containing DNA, provides the continuation of life. Life cannot carry on without blood. To provide life requires life. Life cannot be produced without life. Life is transmitted from the live parents to form the live embryo, the live fetus, and, given time, gives birth to the live baby. If the father of the baby should die before the baby is born, the baby still has a strong chance of experiencing a healthy birth, because the embryo and fetus did not die. The father and mother provided the beginning life of the embryo by planting the live seed at conception. The progressing, growing being is still alive in the mother's womb and will continue to live until it dies.

In the event the cells in the DNA were not kept constantly alive during mating, then the genetic transfer is not possible. This fact proves that life—maintenance of life—is given and sustained at the very moment of conception.

Considering the extreme weakness of an embryo or a fetus:

> God has chosen the weak things of the world to put to shame the things which are mighty.
> (1 Corinthians 1:27b)

What does our God instruct judges to do in cases like this?

> You shall do no injustice in judgment. You shall not be partial to the poor, nor honor the person of the mighty.
> (Leviticus 19:15)

> These things also belong to the wise: It is not good to show partiality in judgment. (Proverbs 24:23)

> You shall not be afraid in any man's presence, for the judgment is God's. The case that is too hard for you, bring to me, and I will hear it. (Deuteronomy 1:17b)

> You shall appoint judges … and they shall judge the people with just judgment. (Deuteronomy 16:18a, c)

We've often heard this plea voiced from the abortion advocates: "It is freedom of choice."

However, we cannot physically hear the fetus say, "I would like freedom to live."

Can a fetus speak up when being judged to die? Are their lives being judged fairly? Does anyone care about those who cannot speak for themselves? Our God does:

> Open your mouth for the speechless, in the cause of all who are appointed to die. Open your mouth, judge righteously. (Proverbs 31:8–9a)

> You shall not show partiality in judgment; you shall hear the small as well as the great. (Deuteronomy 1:17a)

One must wonder if the children in the Old Testament whose lives were sacrificed to false gods were trying to be heard:

> And they caused their sons and daughters to pass through the fire, practiced witchcraft and soothsaying, and sold themselves to do evil in the sight of the LORD to provoke Him to anger. (2 Kings 17:17)

Did anyone hear the children's screams?

> Also he made his son pass through the fire, practiced soothsaying, used witchcraft, and consulted spiritists and mediums. He did much evil in the sight of the LORD to provoke Him to anger. (2 Kings 21:6)

> The Sepharvites burned their children in the fire to Adrammelech and Anammelech, the gods of Sepharvaim. (2 Kings 17:31b)

Also he caused his sons to pass through the fire in the Valley of the Son of Hinnom; he practiced soothsaying, used witchcraft and sorcery, and consulted mediums and spiritists. He did much evil in the sight of the LORD, to provoke Him to anger. (2 Chronicles 33:6)

They served their idols, which became a snare to them. They even sacrificed their sons and their daughters to demons, and shed innocent blood, the blood of their sons and daughters, whom they sacrificed to the idols of Canaan; and the land was polluted with blood. (Psalm 106:36–38a)

Moreover you took your sons and your daughters, whom you bore to Me, and these you sacrificed to them to be devoured. Were your acts of harlotry a small matter, that you have slain My children and offered them up to them by causing them to pass through the fire? (Ezekiel 16:20–21)

For they have committed adultery, and blood is on their hands. They have committed adultery with their idols, and even sacrificed their sons whom they bore to Me, passing them through the fire, to devour them. (Ezekiel 23:37)

The New Testament tells us that those Old Testament examples were written for our learning:

For whatever things were written before were written for our learning, that we through the patience and comfort of the Scriptures might have hope. (Romans 15:4)

Now these things became our examples, to the intent that we should not lust after evil things as they also lusted. (1 Corinthians 10:6)

> Now all these things happened to them as examples, and
> they were written for our admonition, upon whom the
> ends of the ages have come. (1 Corinthians 10:11)

Everything God has to say about abortion is discouraging to any person who supports it. However, here is some exceedingly encouraging news:

In the first three Gospel Books alone, we learn that only God can forgive sins, and we find at least ten times repeated that our Lord Jesus is that God Who forgives. For example:

> Son, be of good cheer; your sins are forgiven you.
> (Matthew 9:2b)

> Son, your sins are forgiven you. (Mark 2:5)

> Then Jesus said to her, "Your sins are forgiven."
> (Luke 7:48)

> Then he said to the woman, "Your faith has saved you."
> (Luke 7:50)

Forgiveness is not something we can see with our eyes or touch with our hands. Forgiveness is the pardon for a fault or offense; when we are forgiven, we are excused from the penalty (like a prison sentence, or an execution, or to be judged to be cast into the eternal Lake of Fire).

The sin of abortion is no lesser or no more than any sin, including the telling of a lie.

> You shall not steal, nor deal falsely, nor lie to one
> another. And you shall not swear by My name falsely,
> nor shall you profane the name of your God: I am the
> LORD. (Leviticus 19:11–12)

All of us have sin nature in our blood. It is in our genes. We have inherited the DNA from our ancestors Adam and Eve. There is nothing we can do about it except to admit our guilt and sincerely ask our God for forgiveness and, with the Spirit's help, turn away from it.

> As it is written: "There is none righteous, no, not one." (Romans 3:10)

> For there is not a just man on earth who does good and does not sin. (Ecclesiastes 7:20)

> For whoever shall keep the whole law, and yet stumble in one point, he is guilty of all. For He who said, "Do not commit adultery," also said, "Do not murder." Now if you do not commit adultery, but you do murder, you have become a transgressor of the law. (James 2:10–11)

The good news is that our Lord Jesus Christ died on the cross, taking our sins upon Himself, dying for us, shedding His blood to forgive us, and on the third day after His death, God raised Him from the dead. He did this to show us that if we repent and believe that Jesus is God—with His Father and with the Holy Spirit—then He will forgive us and also raise us back to life to be with Him in heaven.

> For He made Him who knew no sin to be sin for us,
> that we might become the righteousness of God in Him.
> (2 Corinthians 5:21)

The tiny life that has been aborted is innocent. That means not guilty of any sin—therefore righteous and justified to go to God's kingdom. If a mother who experienced an abortion would like to meet her little one, all things are possible with God.

In regard to this delicate issue, we should consider the even more delicate embryo. We need to listen to God and not rely upon judges or any other people of this world:

> Do not be conformed to this world, but be transformed
> by the renewing of your mind, that you may prove what

is that good and acceptable and perfect will of God. (Romans 12:2)

We've heard mention of the stages of human life. Those are just the physical part. At any time during any one of the phases, we can prematurely be transformed from, say, the fetus, infant, child, teen, adult, middle age, or senior, to the spiritual, eternal phase of our being. And when the Lord returns as He has promised, we will again be in glorified, physical bodies. This is guaranteed:

> For our citizenship is in heaven, from which we also eagerly wait for the Savior, the Lord Jesus Christ, who will transform our lowly body that it may be conformed to His glorious body, according to the working by which He is able even to subdue all things to Himself. (Philippians 3:20-21)

The determining factor of physical life according to God is contained in the blood.

As physical life is inherited from our parents, spiritual life is inherited from our Savior, conceived at the moment our minds and hearts are renewed.

We see this repeated three times in the Book of Leviticus. Here, we see it again:

> The blood is the life. (Deuteronomy 12:23b)

> Therefore choose life, that both you and your descendants may live. (Deuteronomy 30:19b)

Since the Lord Jesus Christ died for us and shed His lifeblood to forgive us and give us eternal life, it could thus be called a spiritual blood transfusion.

The high court judges made it sound as if it is okay to have an abortion. Our God is ready to forgive and forget the sins of even the judges, if they are simply willing to accept His free gift.

> For You, Lord, are good, and ready to forgive, and abundant in mercy to all those who call upon You. Go in peace. (Psalm 86:5)

UNREVISED HISTORY

Educational institutions have recently tampered with historical accounts that have been documented for hundreds of years. Revising history to suit one's opinion is unfair to the younger generations; they don't hear the truth of what actually took place. Revising history keeps us from seeing where we are headed because we aren't looking honestly at where we've been.

The kindergartens, schools, colleges, and universities in North America that teach yoga and sexual orientation but do not allow Bible teaching are being neither tolerant nor inclusive. The founding fathers of America seriously considered freedom of religion in the Declaration of Independence.

The American Civil Liberty Union uses the phrase "separation of church and state" to make efforts in court cases resulting in elimination of anything having to do with Christianity, the Bible, or the Lord Jesus Christ on government properties. But the phrase "separation of church and state" cannot be found in the Constitution of the United States; it cannot be found in the Declaration of Independence; and it cannot be found in the Bill of Rights.

Here is the truth about the phrase: President Thomas Jefferson repeated that phrase in a January 1, 1802, letter he sent to the Danbury Baptist Association.[63] The president's laborious, handwritten draft is included

---

[63] LIBRARY OF CONGRESS, Information Bulletin, June 1998, "Jefferson's Letter to the Danbury Baptists", (May 2019), https://www.loc.gov/loc/lcib/9806/danpre.html

in the government archives. His purpose was to comfort the church to know that the government would not hinder nor interfere and would respect their right to practice their faith. But anti-Christians twisted the simple meaning to suit their own opinion. Following the president's kind introduction, here is the core wording of his letter:

> Believing with you that religion is a matter which lies solely between Man & his God, that he owes account to none other for his faith or his worship, that the legitimate powers of government reach actions only, & not opinions, I contemplate with sovereign reverence that act of the whole American people which declared that their legislature should 'make no law respecting an establishment of religion, or prohibiting the free exercise thereof,' thus building a wall of separation between Church & State. Adhering to this expression of the supreme will of the nation in behalf of the rights of conscience, I shall see with sincere satisfaction the progress of those sentiments which tend to restore to man all his natural rights, convinced he has no natural right in opposition to his social duties.
>
> I reciprocate your kind prayers for the protection & blessing of the common father and creator of man, and tender you for yourselves & your religious association, assurances of my high respect & esteem.
>
> Signed: Th Jefferson

The Declaration of Independence lists twenty-seven facts to prove the absolute tyranny of the King of England, which prompted the absolving of allegiance to the British Crown. Following are only a few examples:

"He" [the King of England] "has refused his assent to laws, the most wholesome and necessary for the public good."

"He [the king] has dissolved Representative Houses repeatedly, for opposing with manly firmness his [the king's] invasions on the rights of the people." (A reminder for the ACLU opposing the rights of the people to have freedom of religion in the ACLU's designated places. Contrast this: The people are not allowed to display a cross or to pray on public property, but elected officials are allowed in public to use their Creator's name in vain.)

"He ([the king] has erected multitudes of new offices, and sent hither swarms of officers to harass our people, and eat out their substance."

"He [the king] has kept among us, in times of peace, Standing Armies without the Consent of our legislatures. He has affected to render the Military independent of and superior to the Civil power. He has combined with others to subject us to a jurisdiction foreign to our constitution, and unacknowledged by our laws; giving his Assent to their Acts of pretended Legislation: For quartering large bodies of armed troops among us."

Children in public schools today are not taught the original reason for the Second Amendment. The citizens stand ready to protect the freedom they have and to preserve it for their offspring (just in case government officials attempt to repeat the king's history).

What we read in President Jefferson's letter and in the Declaration of Independence is reason to say that the court today is already repeating history that caused declaration of spiritual war on the rights and consciences of the people in the first place—a battle that erupted into the Revolutionary War. The thirteen colonies fought and defeated the British Empire, but not without much shed blood and loss of life and limb on both sides. Many modern-day schools no longer teach the history of the battles and heroes like John Paul Jones, Patrick Henry, and George Washington. Historical monuments are being torn down, erasing the history they represent.

Not only do modern-day disrupters attempt to take away our right to freely worship and pray anywhere without hindrance, but they also divide those who were previously united. Nowhere do we reasonably interpret that our rights are revoked if we exercise those rights on government property.

Furthermore, with the rights of which we've been blessed, unbelievers (and even ACLU lawyers) are not coerced into participating in any religion if they have no desire to do so. It is their right to reject the Savior. In fact, our God and Creator gives all of us a free will to do as we please. He does not force Himself onto anyone. Jesus is a Gentleman; if He knocks on a door and the door is not opened, He does not force His way in; He says,

> "Behold, I stand at the door and knock. If anyone hears
> My voice and opens the door, I will come in to him and
> dine with him, and he with Me." (Revelation 3:20)

The very title of the US Bill of Rights says exactly what it is about. It is the rights of the people—not the agenda of the king. The Bill of Rights is the first ten amendments to the US Constitution, and the very first one is the right of the people to have freedom of religion, speech, and the press. Of course it must be recognized that if anyone abuses any of these privileges, then other laws must be enforced. For example, if people think they can become violent protestors and destroy either private or public property, then that is an abuse of the freedom of speech.

It becomes extremely difficult to understand why some are allowed to indoctrinate children and students with opposing views to those of the Christian believers, while simultaneously the sound doctrine of God's Word is attacked and not even allowed, and it's the government—the ACLU—the "king" who is prohibiting it.

The judges need to take a closer look and ask for divine discernment in order to make moral decisions that affect the rights of expressing faith, speech, and press. Each man and woman needs to consider the eternal consequences of not listening.

If you think that the works you've done are good enough to save yourself from the Lake of Fire, the next short passage needs to be understood:

> For by grace you have been saved through faith, and that not of yourselves; it is the gift of God, not of works, lest anyone should boast. (Ephesians 2:8–9)

We cannot boast that we can save ourselves for going to heaven; only the Savior can save us. Since He ascended up into heaven and is not physically present with us, He depends upon His Word in the Bible to now provide the truth that saves:

> For I am not ashamed of the gospel of Christ, for it is the power of God to salvation for everyone who believes. (Romans 1:16a)

Paraphrasing Ephesians 2:10, God's Word tells us we practice doing good works or good deeds—that is, we obey the commands of our God and Savior, the Lord Jesus Christ—not to save ourselves, but rather we do things pleasing to God because He has already saved us. We don't do works to save ourselves; He did the work on the cross.

Jesus answered a Pharisee lawyer who called Him Teacher and asked Him a question to test Him:

> "Teacher, which is the great commandment in the law?" Jesus said to him, "'You shall love the LORD your God with all your heart, with all your soul, and with all your mind.' This is the first and great commandment." (Matthew 22:36–38)

The Gospel according to Mark adds that we are commanded to:

> "'love the LORD your God with all your heart, with all your soul, with all your mind, and with all your strength.'" (Mark 12:30a)

> Jesus answered and said to him, "If anyone loves Me, he will keep My word; and My Father will love him, and We will come to him and make Our home with him." (John 14:23)

We can only express our love in return by being obedient to His commands. Jesus says,

> If you love Me, keep My commandments. (John 14:15)

> He who has My commandments and keeps them, it is he who loves Me. (John 14:21a)

> We love Him because He first loved us. (1 John 4:19)

Our Father loved us so much that He had His Son shed His blood to forgive us and die for us so that we could be raised from being dead and live forever.

No matter how many times we go to church; no matter how many times we take communion; whether we get baptized by man or not; whether we help an elderly lady cross the street; no matter how many things we do which are good things to do, we cannot save ourselves. We are saved only by the grace of God, only by believing, only by our sincere faith and trust in the Savior, trusting that He shed His blood to forgive us of our offenses, died for us in our place, and was raised from the dead back to life for all eternity. This truth is the foundational hope of all Christianity.

None of us can do anything good enough to save ourselves. Being saved by grace means that even though we do not deserve to be saved, God accepts us simply and only because He knows we have truly come to believe in Him.

That's all He asks.

When we believe, then we know His Son, whom He sent to save us, is equally God with Him and with the Holy Spirit.

> Christ Jesus, who, being in the form of God, did not consider it robbery to be equal with God, but made Himself of no reputation, taking the form of a bondservant, and coming in the likeness of men. And being found in appearance as a man, He humbled Himself and became obedient to the point of death, even the death of the cross. (Philippians 2:5b–8)

The gift of grace is free; we cannot pay anything for it. Christ Jesus already paid the tremendous price for us when He took our penalty by dying for us—and as us. Only by our faith, our trust, our belief in Him, are we able to receive our eternal life in heaven.

Grace = G-R-A-C-E: God's Riches At Christ's Expense. Each soul saved by our Savior is viewed by God to be a part of His riches. God is at war with Satan to win our souls. The Lord becomes richer with each victory of gaining a new believer.

* * *

What is the definition of the word *believe*? Someone said, "I'm absolutely positive, I think." That statement leaves room for doubt. In the issue of our faith, believing means becoming fully persuaded, fully convinced of whatever we claim to believe; to know it is absolutely true, with not a shred of doubt; and to know it is indeed absolute truth in one's own heart and mind. Believers believe the Bible—God's Word—to be entirely, utterly true; error-free; without contradiction.

Some people say, "The Bible is the most violent Book I've ever read." Granted, it is a violent thought to picture being nailed high up onto a wooden cross and to bleed and suffocate until death. And granted the Tribulation period in the last Book of the Bible is extremely violent. And there are lots of severe situations in the Old Testament. But there is a vast change of pace from the Old Testament to the New Testament. After four hundred years of God's silence between the Old and New Testaments, all the penalties for our offensive sins against God, and against others, are forgiven simply by our repentance and genuine belief in Him.

God asks no more. Believers, figuratively and spiritually speaking, are His adopted children. He just wants to hear them sincerely say, "Oh, dear Father in heaven, thank You for teaching me to repent; thank You for accepting me, for sending Your Son to forgive me, for saving me, and for giving me eternal life."

For breaking any one of the Ten Commandments, God demands the death of the offender. The New Testament says that the Savior took the violent penalty of death in the believer's place with the result of the believer's eternal life in God's kingdom. God is not partial. His offer is to all sinners, but the life is given only to those who repent, believe, and accept His free offer.

Viewing the Old and New Testaments of the Bible, and quoting Augustine, "The New is in the Old concealed; the Old is in the New revealed."[64] His words (in Latin) have also been translated: "The New is in the Old contained; The Old is in the New explained."[65] The Book of Isaiah in the Old Testament was written in approximately 700 BC:

> All we like sheep have gone astray; we have turned, every one, to his own way; and the LORD [the Father God] has laid on Him [the Son of God] the iniquity of us all. (Isaiah 53:6)

In part of Jesus' first long quoted passage in the Gospel of John, He tells us the Father sends His Son—Jesus Himself—to save us and not to condemn us:

> For God so loved the world [all mankind] that He gave His only begotten Son, that whoever believes in Him should not perish [to the Lake of Fire] but have everlasting life. For God did not send His Son into the

---

[64] Believer's Bible Commentary, William MacDonald, (Thomas Nelson, 1995), "Introduction to the Old Testament", pg 15, 6th paragraph

[65] Believer's Bible Commentary, William MacDonald, (Thomas Nelson, 1995), "Introduction to the Old Testament", pg 20, 6th paragraph

world to condemn the world, but that the world through Him might be saved. He who believes in Him is not condemned; but he who does not believe is condemned already, because he has not believed in the name of the only begotten Son of God. (John 3:16–18)

These are the very first words Mark quoted Jesus, saying,

> "The time is fulfilled, and the kingdom of God is at hand. Repent, and believe in the gospel." (Mark 1:15b)

Luke quotes Jesus near the middle of his Gospel:

> I tell you, no; but unless you repent you will all likewise perish. (Luke 13:3)

> I tell you, no; but unless you repent you will all likewise perish. (Luke 13:5)

One of the most important lessons to learn from the Bible is what's traditionally called the Golden Rule. The New Testament quotes one special Old Testament verse eight times, quoted more times than any other Old Testament verse:

> "You shall love your neighbor as yourself: I am the LORD" (Leviticus 19:18b).

If only the LGBTQ+ community could understand that the Golden Rule is the very reason believers want to bring God's truth to them. We all, believers and unbelievers, have been born with the nature to offend God, because we all are born with Adam's DNA, and this old heart, this blood is what gives us this nature to sin. Christians understand God's unconditional love for all of us, whether we are adulterers, thieves, blasphemers, liars, idolaters, or homosexuals.

God even reminds Christians that they're no better than anyone else. All Christians were in the same darkness, as all of us have offended God, but not necessarily all with the same offenses. But upon believing, the old heart is replaced with a new heart:

> And you [you believers] He [God] made alive, who were dead in trespasses and sins, in which you once walked according to the course of this world, according to the prince of the power of the air [Satan], the spirit who now works in the sons of disobedience, among whom also we all once conducted ourselves in the lusts of our flesh and of the mind, and were by nature children of wrath, just as the others. But God, who is rich in mercy, because of His great love with which He loved us, even when we were dead in trespasses, made us alive together with Christ (by grace you have been saved). (Ephesians 2:1–5)

> But God demonstrates His own love toward us, in that while we were still sinners, Christ died for us. (Romans 5:8)

Christians desire for all to know that believers don't desire to be hypocrites. Rather, believers are trying to transmit and express the unconditional love of God so that all will be saved who hear, absorb, digest, and apply the truth of God's divine plan to save us from eternal suffering in unquenchable fire. He gives eternal life in heaven. Every minute that goes by brings one moment closer to our end on this earth. True Christians live with hope of living for all eternity with the Savior and with our loved ones who are saved.

The word *eternal* needs to capture our utmost attention. Seeking the truth leads to the most important decision of this earthly life. Forever is a long, endless time. No one wants to see anyone suffer for that eternal, never-ending time. None of us are going to get out of this alive. We all need to be prepared.

> Prepare to meet your God. (Amos 4:12b)

Seek the LORD while He may be found, call upon Him
while He is near. (Isaiah 55:6)

For it is time to seek the LORD (Hosea 10:12b)

"Therefore you also be ready, for the Son of Man [Jesus,
who is also the Son of God] is coming at an hour you do
not expect." (Luke 12:40)

* * *

God's plan for building families required that He would create both man
and woman and thereby increase the earth's population.

So God created man in His own image; in the image
of God He created him; male and female He created
them. Then God blessed them, and God said to them,
"Be fruitful and multiply; fill the earth and subdue it;
have dominion over the fish of the sea, over the birds of
the air, and over every living thing that moves on the
earth." (Genesis 1:27–28)

Seven times the Book of Genesis tells that God created all living things
of flesh male and female. Genesis 6:19 quotes God saying it exactly:

And of every living thing of all flesh you shall bring two
of every sort into the ark, to keep them alive with you;
they shall be male and female. (Genesis 6:19)

God instituted marriage between one man and one woman:

Therefore a man shall leave his father and mother and
be joined to his wife, and they shall become one flesh.
(Genesis 2:24)

From the beginning of history, this was, and still is, God's grand plan.

By going against God's divine, natural design, His authority is confronted, but in no way is His power diminished. God does not change (Malachi 3:6).

Be careful, watch out, and do not be deceived.

> Beloved, do not believe every spirit, but test the spirits, whether they are of God; because many false prophets have gone out into the world. (1 John 4:1)

Jesus' disciples asked Him:

> "Tell us, when will these things be? And what will be the sign of Your coming, and of the end of the age?" And Jesus answered and said to them: "Take heed that no one deceives you." (Matthew 24:3b–4; Mark 13:5)

> But of that day and hour no one knows, not even the angels of heaven, but My Father only. (Matthew 24:26; Mark 13:32)

> And He said to them, "It is not for you to know times or seasons which the Father has put in His own authority." (Acts 1:7)

> And He said: "Take heed that you not be deceived: For many will come in My name, saying, 'I am He,' and, 'The time has drawn near.' Therefore do not go after them." (Luke 21:8)

> Do you not know that the unrighteous will not inherit the kingdom of God? Do not be deceived. (1 Corinthians 6:9a)

> Do not be deceived: "Evil company corrupts good habits." (1 Corinthians 15:33)

> The righteous should choose his friends carefully, for the way of the wicked leads them astray. (Proverbs 12:26)

He who walks with wise men will be wise, but the companion of fools will be destroyed. (Proverbs 13:20)

Therefore let him who thinks he stands take heed lest he fall. (1 Corinthians 10:12)

Do not be deceived, God is not mocked; for whatever a man sows, that he will also reap. (Galatians 6:7)

But evil men and impostors will grow worse and worse, deceiving and being deceived. (2 Timothy 3:13)

Let no one say when he is tempted, "I am tempted by God"; for God cannot be tempted by evil, nor does He Himself tempt anyone. But each one is tempted when he is drawn away by his own desires and enticed. Then, when desire has conceived, it gives birth to sin; and sin, when it is full-grown, brings forth death. Do not be deceived, my beloved brethren. Every good gift and every perfect gift is from above, and comes down from the Father of lights, with whom there is no variation or shadow of turning. (James 1:13–17)

But there were also false prophets among the people, even as there will be false teachers among you, who will secretly bring in destructive heresies, even denying the Lord who bought them, and bring on themselves swift destruction. (2 Peter 2:1)

But the day of the Lord will come as a thief in the night, in which the heavens will pass away with a great noise, and the elements will melt with fervent heat; both the earth and the works that are in it will be burned up. Therefore, since all these things will be dissolved, what manner of persons ought you to be in holy conduct and godliness? (2 Peter 3:10–11)

For we ourselves were also once foolish, disobedient, deceived, serving various lusts and pleasures, living in malice and envy, hateful and hating one another. (Titus 3:3)

Considering Creation

It is amazing to take note of the human body: two ears formed with curves to catch sound waves; two eyes to see and detect each person by their distinctive looks; one mouth with which to speak, sing, and communicate; a brain with which to learn, record, repeat, and discern whether ideas are factually true; facial skin that changes to flexible lips surrounding the mouth for sealing drink and food; teeth for the initial digestive process; valves for separating food for the stomach or air for the lungs, and so much more. The body can even heal a bleeding cut by the coagulation of blood. And each body has its very own fingerprints, its own DNA characteristics, and its own unique eyeballs.

And doesn't it just feel wonderful to take in a big, deep breath of fresh air? The earth's atmosphere contains air consisting of oxygen, nitrogen, and carbon dioxide.

The sun is at an average distance of about 93 million miles (150 million kilometers) away from earth.[66]

The earth's average orbital speed around the sun is about 67,000 miles per hour, or 110,000 kilometers per hour. The average speed of the earth's daily rotation is 1,000 miles per hour, or about 1,600 kilometers per hour.[67]

---

[66] Cool Cosmos is an IPAC website. Based on Government Sponsored Research NAS7-03001 and NNN12AA01C, "How far away is the Sun?", 1st sentence (December 2019) http://coolcosmos.lpac.caltech.edu/ask/8-How-far-away-is-the-Sun-

[67] Cornell University, "Our Solar System – The Earth- Orbit", (December 2019) http://curious.astro.cornell.edu/about-us/41-our-solar-system/the-earth/orbit/91-at-what-speed-does-the-earth-move-around-the-sun-beginner

At the equator, the circumference of the earth is 40,070 kilometers, and the day is twenty-four hours long, so the speed is 1,670 kilometers per hour (1,037 miles per hour).[68]

Our Creator, Jesus Christ, holds everything together even while it is all constantly in motion. The *Choice Gleanings Calendar* for Saturday, June 22, 2019, had this to say: "In Him all things consist" (Colossians 1:17).

The commentary by W. Ross Rainey reads, "When we think of Christ's controlling and unifying power in the universe, consider that planet earth is moving in four different ways at once. It is rotating on its axis at 29 miles a second (at the equator); it is circling around the sun at 19 miles a second; it is moving with the solar system around the Milky Way at 170 miles a second—all as the universe expands outward."

This hymn by Carl Boberg (1859-1940) is then given:

> O Lord, my God, when I in awesome wonder,
> Consider all the worlds Thy hands have made,
> O see the stars, I hear the rolling thunder,
> Thy power throughout the universe displayed;
> Then sings my soul, my Savior God, to Thee;
> How great Thou art, how great Thou art!

It is amazing that people and animals can have the ability to stand up straight and even stand still. There is just the right amount of gravity to allow balance, walking, running, and jumping. With the four seasons, there are just the right limits of temperatures to withstand heat and cold, or to experience comfort in between. The stars are always in the same places at expected times. On a dark, clear, moonless night, it is spectacular to view the Milky Way, the Big Dipper, the North Star, the Southern Cross, the Little Dipper, Pleiades, Orion's Belt, and other celestial formations.

---

[68] National Aeronautics and Space Administration, "Ask the Space Scientist – What is the speed of the Earth's rotation?", (June 2019) https://image.gsfc.nasa.gov/poetry/ask/a10840.html

THE heavens declare the glory of God; and the firmament shows His handiwork. (Psalm 19:1)

Considering Wisdom

All the rivers run into the sea, yet the sea is not full; to the place from which the rivers come, there they return again. (Ecclesiastes 1:7)

The true believing Christian who genuinely believes in God and His Word will, come what may, faithfully remain peaceful. The only way that peace for all could ever be achieved is if everyone goes by the same standard; that standard would have to be of sound advice. The available Source that fits this need is sound doctrine. If some are indoctrinated by variable notions of people in this world, and the rest are indoctrinated by God's Word—the Bible—then there will never be peace for all. But for those who are truly listening to their Maker, they are united, and there is peace among them—and with Him. However, God has a plan, and He knows the majority of His creation to whom He gives freedom will continue to reject the Lord Jesus Christ, the Savior. Therefore, those who fail to acknowledge their Creator will never achieve peace.

Oh, the depth of the riches both of the wisdom and knowledge of God! How unsearchable are His judgments and His ways past finding out! (Romans 11:33)

But of Him you are in Christ Jesus, who became for us wisdom from God— (1 Corinthians 1:30a)

Justice and mercy meet at the cross.

Books by Michael Copple

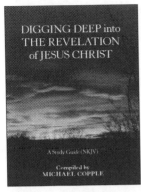

Digging Deep into the Revelation of Jesus Christ
A Study Guide
ISBN: 978-1-9736-4917-5 (sc)
ISBN: 978-1-9736-4916-8 (e)

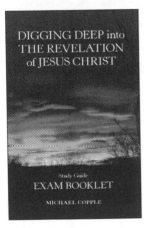

Digging Deep into the Revelation of Jesus Christ
Exam Booklet
ISBN: 978-1-9736-9120-4 (sc)
ISBN: 978-1-9736-9121-1 (e)

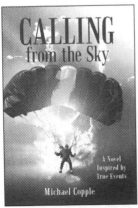

Calling from the Sky
ISBN: 978-1-9736-6903-6 (sc)
ISBN: 978-1-9736-6904-3 (hc)
ISBN: 978-1-9736-6902-9 (e)

04167802-00967071

Printed in the United States
By Bookmasters